Transcending the Elegant Charade

A Guide to Enlightenment & Nondual Consciousness

Transcending The Elegant Charade

A Guide to Enlightenment & Nondual Consciousness

Michael T. Ness

Aperion Books
www.AperionBooks.com

APERION BOOKS™
1611A South Melrose Dr #173
Vista, California 92081
www.AperionBooks.com

10 9 8 7 6 5 4 3 2
First edition
Printed in the United States of America

ISBN-10: 0-9829678-6-1
ISBN-13: 978-0-9829678-6-7
Library of Congress Catalog Card Number: 2011906155

Cover & book design by CenterPointe Media
www.CenterPointeMedia.com

"I am the flame itself
illuminating the shadows of this dream.
Flames leap higher
for every layer that is consumed;
flames dancing in ecstasy,
burning everything unreal."

—FROM *I AM*

Table of Contents

Introduction

The book that you hold in your hands is my attempt to illustrate what I have found to be the most direct path to enlightenment, or nondual consciousness, as many people are calling it these days. I felt compelled to write about the spiritual journey because it is undoubtedly the most important endeavor that any individual can undertake in their lifetime. I have been pursuing this goal indirectly and halfheartedly for nearly twenty years, but about a year ago my life took a turn that thrust me into the fires of this pursuit head long, giving me a most intimate experience of the process.

The method that I have found to be the most direct path to enlightenment is called self-enquiry and it will be detailed throughout this book and especially in the last chapter. I recognize that there are many valid paths to the goal of enlightenment. What I would ask is that you compare whatever path you are utilizing to self-enquiry. If you look closely you will see that all paths resemble self-enquiry when boiled down to their barest essence and most refined state. Several newer authors on the subject of self realization have created their own techniques which they place a clever name on and then present as their own brain child, but most are really just modifications of this most tried and true method. I believe therefore, that no matter what your background or spiritual path, a thorough examination of self-enquiry can only serve to help you clarify and make more effective your own spiritual practice.

The pursuit of enlightenment is fundamentally at the core of all religious and spiritual traditions. In the end we are all looking for peace, grace, love or God; no matter what you call it, we are all looking for the same thing. For the purposes of this book I will be terming God, "Mother Consciousness" or "Absolute Reality," and our abidance in God, "enlightenment" or interchangeably, "nondual consciousness".

For as long as I can remember the question for me has only ever been how to pursue this truth most directly; how to seek it most authentically. This book is a description of my personal process and the insights I've had along the way. Anyone on an authentic spiritual path is searching for this Absolute Reality and so I have endeavored to contribute to our collective search with my own elucidation of a path that I believe must, first and foremost, always lead inward.

Enter the Ego

EARTH FIRE HANDS

Those earth-fire hands
rip through these masks
that tentatively cover
the immensity of soul.
This mind and body
dissolve into consciousness;
lower into higher,
they are one and the same.
All highs and lows are
embraced in this moment;
this is where the real dance unfolds.
Arms and legs moving,
in rhythm around this fire,
we dance while the ego mask burns.

Consciousness is all there is and we are that. That's pretty much the gist of it. Whether you call it God, Buddha, Allah or Shiva, in the final analysis, everything is only One. I wanted to put this statement right out there in order to set the stage for our journey. If you already abide fully in the experience of the truth of nondual consciousness congratulations; I'm sure you've been working towards enlightenment for a long time. If you're not experiencing what I'm talking about, or if you are but the experience is still getting clearer and being refined, then there remains some exploring and explaining to do. Using words for explaining nondual consciousness is challenging because words like consciousness can't be adequately defined and what we really are is most certainly not a "this" or a "that". Even the statement "I Am," the most perfect name for God/Absolute Reality, is only a handy pointer. But used correctly good pointers can lead you to the unassailable experience of nondual consciousness that lies inward, just on the other side of your mind.

Perhaps the only thing that can be truly stated about the nature of Absolute Reality is…nothing. NO THING. We know that we exist; we know that reality exists, but what is the nature of reality itself? What is the bottom line core of existence? This is the most important question of all because in the experience of the answer, lies the key to resolving personal suffering in every sense. Whether your apparent problems have to do with relationships, finances, career, health, self esteem or lack of authentic Chinese restaurants in your area, in the experience of nondual consciousness you will find the ultimate resolution.

Nondual consciousness is the ultimate modus operandi that rectifies all the seeming discrepancies of the dualistic world. In truth, Absolute Reality is one unified consciousness that only appears to be ever shifting and changing. It appears to be divided up into temporary phenomenon such as our individual self, other people, places, things and life situations, but herein lay the trap. Once we've mentally divided the world up into better and worse, we tend to try to hold onto specific moments in time, thought patterns, personal possessions, certain situations and special relationships, only to eventually be disappointed when they change. We all know the world changes, but still we try to compartmentalize life and freeze dry our favorite bits to keep them eternally fresh. We pine for and grasp at life's highs and attempt to repel life's lows. Simply stated, if you identify with and are emotionally tied into any of the changing appearances of reality you will suffer. Suffering is inevitable to the extent that you require events or situations to transpire in a particular manner or to remain in a particular shape. Perhaps in your youth you managed to climb to the top of Mount Kilimanjaro with a wounded alpaca on your shoulders. So what? Get over it. You don't want to be that *one* guy in the retirement home telling the same old tired story while somebody feeds you pudding.

"When viewed from a nondual perspective, reality simply is what it is: it is all inclusive, perfect, complete, and always in the here and now."

If in each moment of life, you can see beyond the temporary phenomenon; if you can continuously identify with the entirety of unified nondual consciousness, you will always be at peace. You will be at peace because you will no longer be tied into specific outcomes in your life. You will exist seamlessly in the moment and have no thought for the future or the past. The details of each moment become just a beautiful reminder, each one pointing toward the absolute perfection and entirety of the whole. When viewed from a nondual perspective, reality simply is what it is: it is all inclusive, perfect, complete, and always in the here and now.

Absolute Reality—God—Mother Consciousness; can be considered the totality of all that IS in this moment. I define nondual consciousness as the undivided, unrestricted experience of this Absolute Reality. To try and paint a picture of the experience of Absolute Reality in words would be a fool's errand and an impossible task. It is impossible because Absolute Reality is the place where all pictures disappear and all words revert to utter silence. What I will be endeavoring to do rather, is to shed light on and to dissect what it is that holds most people back from the experience of reality *as it is*. This book is a guide to help you get your bearings on the road, and to avoid the pitfalls on the journey to a successful personal discovery of Absolute Reality as experienced through nondual consciousness.

In a moment we will be bringing to center stage what it is that holds each of us back from the experience of nondual consciousness and Absolute Reality. Even though it doesn't like to be looked at much less examined closely, I would like to present, hailing from your own imagination; the fantastic, enchanting, elusive, sometimes downright ugly, mean and nasty human ego.

But first, a little bit of back story...

I had my first real glimpse of reality tripping on acid at the beach when I was 19 or 20 years old. Kind of cliché I know, but my tenuous paradigm of reality was transcended in those moments; not blown away entirely, but unhinged for a few blissful hours. I stood at the end of a jetty in Hermosa Beach, California, watching the sun rise and the ocean swelling and breathing all around me. I felt the barriers between self and surroundings lift and had a small, fleeting taste of a nondual state.

During that short time I knew with absolute certainty that all was well, that reality was one unified whole; that it always had been and it always would be perfect. For the first time in years I didn't feel false or out of place. I felt perfectly right, whole, complete and at peace. It occurred to me that it was odd that I should find it so refreshing, strange and peculiar to feel absolutely at one with the universe.

I understood in those moments why the American hippy culture of the 60's made such a push to shift the cultural paradigm toward peace and love. They understood that the pervading cultural paradigm of the day was firmly rooted in a false dichotomy. In the nondual state that I was experiencing, my mind was bypassed and I experienced an all pervasive feeling that I could only describe as unconditional love. My heart was overwhelmed, my capacity for feeling had been pushed beyond its limits and I became love itself. In those moments I was fundamentally at one with the entirety of the universe. In that state there was only this blissful perfection that went far beyond what I normally experienced as the limitations of my body and mind; far beyond my everyday reality. Concepts like greed, hatred, fear and regret had no meaning in a paradigm without boundaries. What could I hate when I was everything? What could I fear when there was only myself? I threw my arms into the sky in a gesture of rapture, love and bliss. I was the alpha and the omega, one without a second! I knew without a doubt that everything was God.

A few hours later, after the drugs wore off, I understood why the hippy counter culture of the 60's had failed to shift the cultural paradigm all that much. Not enough of them had managed to make the ultimate paradigm shift in a permanent fashion for themselves. Not enough of them had been able to transcend duality completely without the aid of drugs. As the acid wore off and my cognitive restraints snapped efficiently back into place, I panicked. I looked at my hands and they seemed to belong to somebody else. They looked like fake props that were for some reason unbeknownst to me, floating in my very near proximity and with obvious ill intentions. I looked down and noticed there were legs there too. I wasn't quite sure what to make of the situation or how to proceed. My brain kicked into gear and I realized I had to get home and get some sleep before I went to work making pizzas. I had exams to study for and I wasn't sure if I was still capable of reading or even coherent thought. At that time I was still living with my parents while going to college, and wondered how I was going to sneak through the front door and into my room. I figured I must have looked like an alien creature with insanity radiating from my eyeballs in all directions. I had gone from blissed out unity consciousness, to feeling like my body was some kind of strange, uncomfortable, dirty flesh costume that didn't really belong to me and yet, that I couldn't get away from.

From that day on I felt a dire need to tear asunder the façade of separation, to go beyond my cognitive restraints and to transcend my ego/mind entirely. I made an agreement with myself and with Mother Consciousness on that day that I would find a way to experience her Absolute Reality in a permanent fashion and without drugs. I *needed* to experience nondual consciousness as fully and continuously as possible. Nondual consciousness was the ultimate paradigm and I had been granted a fleeting taste. Having glimpsed my true nature there was nothing else that could really ever satiate me again. Now 20 years later, after much drama and comedy and having traversed many paths toward the goal, I have finally found the key to what I've always been looking for and which has been here all along. Although I do not lay claim to having had an "absolute awakening," I've been ushered into a nearly continual experience of the divinity and perfection of all things; into a more stable experience of Absolute Reality than ever before. The flow of nondual consciousness has become steady, reliable, open and free; leaving me in a state where thoughts and emotions are fleeting, and where a perfect sense of well being is the norm.

"Though Absolute Reality is our fundamental core, it cannot be experienced fully and directly until the ego mask has been thoroughly dismantled."

Nondual consciousness is the experience of our true nature. It is our connection to and experience of Mother Consciousness: Absolute Reality. For most of us however, our true nature is covered up with a complex conglomeration of ideas, beliefs and emotions that comprise a false individual identity. This false identity is what I refer to as the ego mask. Though Absolute Reality is our fundamental core, it cannot be experienced fully and directly until the ego mask has been thoroughly dismantled. Dismantling the ego mask however, is no easy task. Sufficient impetus is required to even begin to move toward this unraveling and in my experience, this impetus is difficult to generate without some prolonged mental and emotional suffering or dissatisfaction. It is difficult to even *want* to break free from the illusory dualistic world until you've realized the utter futility of thrashing about in a life in a world that is ultimately a dream.

My path to nondual consciousness was not the pretty, lovey-dovey sweet smelling stuff they sell you in the new-age shops. For destroying the ego no incense or magical crystals are required. When awakening came for me it was jarring. It was brutal. It was an identity crisis that felt like a punishment bestowed by the mighty hammer of Thor directly onto my already dried and cracking ego mask. My ego mask didn't just get chipped this time, it got pulverized. I was, over the period of a year, compelled by a series of life events to critically examine every aspect of myself that held me back from the experience of Absolute Reality. I had hard questions, likely the same questions that all spiritual seekers must end up asking one day. I wanted to understand the nature of suffering and I wanted to understand it thoroughly. What was holding me back from the experience of what I knew in my heart to be my true nature: abiding peace and happiness? I was compelled not just to look at my suffering, but to gaze at it piercingly. I endeavored to tear it apart until I had unraveled it, pulled out its guts and understood all of its mysteries completely.

The introspective method that I utilized—self-enquiry—is a very direct process in which one continually examines the nature of one's conscious awareness. Emotional suffering, it seems, can lend a crucial force to one's self-enquiry and actually serve to accelerate the process of ego annihilation. It is an introspective tool which one can use to strip away the false aspects of self until only nondual consciousness remains.

Self-enquiry is the most direct method that I know of to attain nondual consciousness. It is a method that has been handed down from ancient times in the tradition of Advaita Vedanta. It was most recently popularized by Ramana Maharshi[1]: one of the most well known, truth realized masters of 20th century India. Self-enquiry along with one pointed effort, fueled by emotional suffering, allowed me to rip through layers of ego with a greater deal of ferocity than I could have mustered had all my life circumstances been peachy keen.

Emotional suffering may not be the main incentive for pursuing ego dissolution for everyone, but I believe it is what generates the motivation for most. The first step to freedom generally involves utter dissatisfaction with the world of duality. You get fed up when you begin to realize that for every good thing that has ever happened in your life, you've undergone an equally crappy thing. You'll start to acknowledge that your ego has had you bouncing around your life emotionally, toward this and away from that, like a rubber ball for as long as you can remember and you're tired of it. Perhaps you'll just be meandering through your life complacently when some negative external circumstances force you to go inward and begin to fiercely question the nature of reality. If you continue to look at it closely, the world of duality will eventually reveal itself as the redundant cosmic joke that it is.

Perhaps it is possible to muster the impetus to unravel the ego fully in the absence of negative life experiences or emotional suffering, but I believe that is rare. Though there are accounts of a handful of sages who were "ripe" and simply burst into nondual consciousness

---

[1] Sri Ramana Maharshi (December 30, 1879—April 14, 1950), born Venkataraman Iyer, was a Hindu sage. He was born to a Tamil-speaking Brahmin family in Tiruchuzhi, Tamil Nadu. After having attained liberation at the age of 16, he left home for Arunachala, a mountain considered sacred by Hindus, at Tiruvannamalai, and lived there for the rest of his life. Although born a Brahmin, after having attained *moksha* he declared himself an "*Atiasrami*," a *Sastraic* state of nonattachment to anything in life and beyond all caste restrictions[1]. The ashram that grew around him, Sri Ramanasramam is situated at the foothill of Arunachala, to the west to the pilgrimage town of Tiruvannamalai.

as children or teenagers e.g. Ramana Maharshi, this appears to be very much the exception rather than the rule. In my experience, the spiritual quest does not begin in earnest for most of us until well after we have already been matriculated into the world of duality and thus set up inevitably for emotional suffering.

The first noble truth of Buddhism[2] states that life is suffering. Lived from the vantage point of the ego this is true. To go beyond suffering and eliminate the possibility of future suffering, one must transcend the ego and therefore the world of duality altogether. The perception of and belief in duality is the only real falsity there is. By duality I mean the artificial divisions we foist upon the world and life like better/worse, easy/hard, me/you, work/play, rich/poor, etc. If the doorbell rings and we open the door to find a leprechaun bearing a pot of gold this is good. If the doorbell rings and we open the door to find

---

[2] In the Theravada version and the version translated by An Shigao, the Four Noble Truths are given definitions:
1. The Nature of Suffering (or *Dukkha*): "This is the noble truth of suffering: birth is suffering, aging is suffering, illness is suffering, death is suffering; sorrow, lamentation, pain, grief and despair are suffering; union with what is displeasing is suffering; separation from what is pleasing is suffering; not to get what one wants is suffering; in brief, the five aggregates subject to clinging are suffering."[4][5]
2. Suffering's Origin (*Dukkha Samudaya*): "This is the noble truth of the origin of suffering: it is this craving which leads to renewed existence, accompanied by delight and lust, seeking delight here and there, that is, craving for sensual pleasures, craving for existence, craving for extermination."[4][5]
3. Suffering's Cessation (*Dukkha Nirodha*): "This is the noble truth of the cessation of suffering: it is the remainderless fading away and cessation of that same craving, the giving up and relinquishing of it, freedom from it, nonreliance on it."[4][5]
4. The Path (*Dukkha Nirodha Gamini Patipada Magga*) Leading to the Cessation of Suffering: "This is the noble truth of the way leading to the cessation of suffering: it is the Noble Eightfold Path; that is, right view, right intention, right speech, right action, right livelihood, right effort, right mindfulness and right concentration."[6][7]

nobody there and a flaming bag of dog crap on the porch, this is bad. If our retirement plan is all spic and span this is good. If we loose our job and become homeless this is bad. If our health is robust and we jog five miles every day, this is good. If we get in a car accident and lose a leg, this is bad. The examples are endless, but the fact remains: this is and always has been a world of ups and downs, and it would be hard to want to annihilate the ego if our duality was going particularly well.

If you've never had a sufficient dose of suffering in your life, the world of duality will probably remain appealing until you do. The reason for this is simple: the ego is quite content to tow the party line when it is getting everything that it wants. It is only when things begin to take a turn for the worse that the ego rails and begins to exhibit fear, hostility, anger and a host of other negative emotions. This is when it is easiest to observe the nasty ego in action: when it is no longer comfortable and appeased and begins rearing its ugly head. It is precisely when the ego is provoked and trashing about, that it can be clearly seen that it is this hideous construct—which has nothing to do with our true nature—that is holding us back from Absolute Reality. However you manage to generate the impetus, the process of ego dissolution and the transcending of duality takes tremendous energy and an unwavering dedication to find truth at all cost.

The perception of and belief in duality is continually perpetuated by the limited view from the ego mask. In essence, the ego mask is what delineates us as individual entities, separate from the rest of the world. The ego mask is comprised of layers upon layers of artifice that create the illusion of autonomy, and not until you've painfully whittled the crust down to the innermost layer, can the truth of who you really are begin to shine through. Most spiritual practices and minor life crises only ever chip the ego mask a little bit, but left to its own devices, the mind is a master of recalibrating and reassembling the ego mask rather quickly.

We begin to create the artificial mask-like ego construct in partnership with our parents and society the moment we are born. It is the barrier that we create and hold up between ourselves and the rest of the universe in order to assert our individuality. It is the illusory construct that separates us from the rest of the universe and keeps the worldly game afoot. It is the limited paradigm that allows for all the evil and injustice that appear to exist in this world.

"As the mask continues to take shape we continue to temper it in the fire of life experience."

Gender and name are some of the first things to be attributed to the tiny bundle of instincts, desires and genetic tendencies that we call an infant. Later we begin to add ideas of ethnicity, rules of family dynamics, ideas of right and wrong, societal expectations, religion, economic status etc. into the mix. These basic ideas are combined and we start to generate more abstract ideas like perceived strengths and weaknesses and personal opinions.

Once these concepts have been combined and stirred together properly, we dip our finger in, bring it to our lips and begin to taste our goals, desires and ambitions, worries and regrets and an endless amount of emotional variations of hope and fear. Where family and society had got the ball rolling for us, we accommodate and begin caking this pasty conglomeration of ideas over our consciousness to form a rudimentary mask. We continue to layer the thick paste together, adding consistency here, decorations and style there, shaping it all the while, until it is substantial enough to make us feel comfortable and safe. As the mask continues to take shape we continue to temper it in the fire of life experience. After a certain point of development, when it has been imbued with a sufficient amount of energy, the ego mask seemingly even takes on a life of its own.

As children, the first thing we begin to understand is our name. I'm Michael and that differentiates me from you and the rest of the world. We begin to recognize our parents as very important and special individuals. We begin to learn the meanings of more extended family relationships. We begin to understand the difference between boys and girls; that boys should be like x,y,z and girls should be like a,b,c. Using these basic markers we create our mask with an infinite number of possible variations. We might identify strongly with our family, friends, ethnicity, nationality, religion or even various sports teams. Maybe it is our personal relationships that make up the better part of our mask. Perhaps our career is what we will base a lot of our identity on. It is an interesting observation that within minutes of meeting someone in our society, they will often ask you, "So what do you do?" Career is one of the foremost definitions that people use to categorize themselves and others in western society, and people are judged primarily by what they do rather than what they fundamentally are.

In our society, most of us have built comfortably fitting, thick, crusty ego masks by the time we hit our teens. Most of us then spend the remainder of our lives upholding, tempering and perfecting our ego masks. We surround ourselves with others who agree to tell us how sturdy and good looking our mask is if only we will reciprocate the favor. We end up huddled together, like little bubbles on a crashing wave, isolated into little niches in a falsely segmented society.

During our adolescence and teens we believe we are trying to find our true identity, but the irony is we are really creating a false identity; defining and solidifying our mask to shield us from the fear of an ever changing, infinite reality. Perhaps we become high school jocks or cheerleaders and we only hang out with the kids who belong to our clique. Maybe we are in the punk rock crowd and we think the jocks and cheerleaders are morons. Regardless of the form, we are always looking for a stable mental and social framework to protect us from the vastness of eternity, but ultimately it cannot be done. Every which way we strive to identify ourselves solidifies the ego mask a little bit more and alienates us further from Absolute Reality. Even the most rebellious display of teenage angst is really only another way to give the ego mask more definition by pitting it against other egos.

If, as teenagers, our parents listen to country we might decide to become fans of death metal. If we look around and see that every one else has brown or black or blonde hair, we might decide to dye our hair purple or blue etc. It becomes part of our nostalgic story and we tell others how as teenagers, we dyed our hair multiple colors, got a nipple ring and flipped off the world with both hands. We build up and refine our ego masks in an effort to create a fortress, to cultivate a feeling of safety and to push back a lingering fear that we can't escape and can never quite define.

What we fail to realize in the beginning is that absolute freedom from duality is the only real safety there is, and it cannot be had while wearing a mask. Our ego masks are what we use to try and solidify our place in a temporary world. The duality of the world is the fundamental illusion that is transcended when the ego mask is destroyed and consciousness is completely uncovered. Pure consciousness, unfettered and shining perfectly is our true birth right, yet strangely we've constructed a world in which experiencing this reality is extremely rare. We've made up a game with rules that dictate that enlightenment is difficult to attain and heaven is someplace far away in a different time. Perhaps we have been taught that there is only one particular religion that God condones and that we must follow it to attain eternal salvation. Adding religious or spiritual beliefs and ideas to our already shrouded consciousness however, is like painting religious or spiritual markings on our mask. We are decorating our masks rather than doing the only sane thing there is: smashing the mask into tiny pieces.

The mind can use an infinite number of strategies to keep the ego mask intact and to keep us enmeshed in the game of duality. Only when we get tired of playing entirely do we start to question and inspect the ego; to start peering at what's behind the mask. Perhaps we pull a card from the game deck of life that says: *Get in a car wreck. Lose your job. Get evicted from your apartment and have a pigeon crap on your head on your way to the welfare line.* It's those kinds of circumstances that get you to questioning the nature of reality very quickly.

"Hey," you'll say, "How come my mask is getting crapped on? Why isn't God taking care of my mask properly? How can this be happening when I pray routinely, chant my mantras and catch and release spiders I find in the house with tiny Tupperware?"

Rarely do you start to question the nature of reality when you pull a card that says: *Make 20 million dollars a year as a professional athlete, marry a supermodel, retire from your charmed career and get cast on Dancing with the Celebrities!*

"Hey," you'd say, "Check out my mask now! Look at all these things I have. I was really cool before, but now that I've got these diamond studs on the forehead of my mask, I'm seriously the man!"

If you're on a spiritual path, a real spiritual path, sooner or later you will begin eying your ego mask very suspiciously. An inner knowing will clue you in to the fact that there is an imposter running around claiming itself to be you. Not only is this imposter brazenly acting and saying things on your behalf, the imposter is doing it right in front of your own eyes and you are the one who gave it the authorization. You'll vaguely remember how you gradually constructed this imposter—the ego mask—and you'll marvel at how audaciously the imposter has broken rank and taken over your entire life. You'll wonder how the heck this imposter has gotten away with the charade for so long. Your entire life this imposter has conspired with the other imposters to fool you into thinking that family role, career, health and economic status are all important for your identification. How come you have always just gone along with this game and never stopped to question if it was necessary or if these ideas were even true?

You'll begin to question the ego imposter when you feel an utter discontentment with the dualistic worldly charade. You get the feeling that the whole universe has been pulling the wool over your eyes.

> "An inner knowing will clue you in to the fact that there is an imposter running around claiming itself to be you."

You begin to intuit that you have a birthright of total freedom that has been denied to you by your entire culture and which you will do anything, absolutely anything to reclaim. The disillusionment stems from a gnawing dissatisfaction that cannot be quelled by anything in this world and becomes too glaringly apparent to ignore. You'll start questioning the foundation of the ego mask and the thoughts that hold it in place. You will wonder why you have been trained to identify yourself with your political party, your age and your marital status. You will ruthlessly begin to question everything you believe and in so doing, you will inevitably be reduced to a shell of the thick ego mask you once were; and inevitably one day...Crack! The shell will get pulverized and what you'll find is that there is nothing inside. Never has been and never will be. You are NO THING. Nondual consciousness exists free and unrestrained, and the ego mask only existed as a self limiting figment of your imagination. It was a self created mask that was required to gain entry into the masquerade ball of life: the elegant charade. And once you gained entry, you sat back and allowed the ego mask to take on a life of its own and evolve into a seemingly autonomous entity.

How beautiful it is to finally unmask; how contrary to the vast majority of the world that is suffering or enjoying or loving or hating life. How natural and liberating nothingness is compared to the frenzy of people struggling to uphold their ego mask; trying to become something better, stronger, prettier, or even something more spiritual. The smashing of the mask is one's only ticket to freedom. It is the gateway to moksha[3] (final liberation). It is liberation from the confines of a stifling, limited mask into pure nondual consciousness and the experience of Absolute Reality. The experience of Absolute Reality through nondual consciousness is synonymous with what some people

---

[3] In Indian religions, Moksha or Mukti, literally "release" (both from a root muc "to let loose, let go"), is the liberation from samsara and the concomitant suffering involved in being subject to the cycle of repeated death and rebirth (reincarnation).

term enlightenment, self realization or truth realization.

If you are utterly disillusioned and ready to do whatever it takes to smash the mask and pull back the curtain, enlightenment will come quickly. If you only have a tiny misgiving that something isn't quite right, you might go on living a life of quiet desperation for decades; one foot in the game and one foot out. If you are completely satisfied that the world as you know it is real and everything is going your way, you might never generate any impetus strong enough to fuel a genuine pursuit of spiritual truth. This is fine. There's no rush. But as long as you're stuck on the roller coaster ride of duality, know that sooner or later your ego mask is going to get cracked.

Chapter Two

Maya's Stick

THE LONELY ROAD TO FREEDOM

The loneliest road that exists
leads away from your futile games.
One by lonely one we must someday
retreat from your deception.
Your cruel, manipulative hands
with painted fingernails
grab people's minds and squeeze,
until the pain becomes too much to bear.
One by lonely one we will
escape from your merry mad house.
I can think of no better time than right now
to bid you farewell.

Maya is a Sanskrit term that can be translated as illusion. In the final analysis, the dualistic world that we occupy is illusory due to its temporary nature. People that are focused on and whose happiness is dependent on outcomes and situations in a temporary dualistic world will eventually experience pain. Such a life must be painful because all circumstances must change. We are happy when times are good and sad when things don't go our way. We are up and down like a yo-yo as long as we are tied into Maya's game. Maya is the personification of the illusory, temporary, dualistic world and if you fall in love with her she'll eventually break your heart.

As long as you hold onto the idea of being someone special in the world you will be subject to the dangers of a transitional existence and on some level living in fear. As long as you wear an ego mask the fear of dissolution will be there lingering, waiting to be triggered. Perhaps the wrinkles that are appearing ever more frequently on your face and the knowledge that you can't stop aging will begin to increase the fear. Maybe your stock portfolio will start fluctuating wildly in an unstable market and you'll worry that your financial future might not be secure. Perhaps it will be a diagnosis of cancer or the death of a loved one that starts the unraveling of your mask. Death is the premier motivator for a journey toward Absolute Reality. Whatever it is that you are tied into emotionally in this world is only temporary and therefore subject to dissolution. The world itself is temporary and must eventually let you down. Even if it never does, *you'll* have to let it go when you die.

Being an ego mask in the world is a bit like being a piñata. To be someone in particular in the world is to hang your mask on the tree of life and go twirling around, hoping not to run into anything hard. But deep down you know there's something out there, something that is making a fearful swooshing noise as it barely misses the edge of your mask time and again. It is something that you hope to never encounter but is impossible to avoid. It is Maya's stick and sooner or later everyone with a mask will get beaten.

If you are something or someone in particular, tied into the outcomes of this world, you are an ego piñata dangling from a tree. Have no doubt that Maya will eventually beat your ass until one day you break open and nothing comes out. Maya will beat your piñata like a child with a voracious sweet tooth. Her candy is emotion and she beats you in order to feed on your fear, anger, sadness, despair and even your hope and joy. It is her job to beat all the dangling ego piñatas: the smug ones, the scared ones, the brave ones and especially the self righteous ones. Maya rolls up her sleeves for the self righteous ones; indignation is one of her very favorite treats. Maya will beat you mercilessly until there is no more candy left for her. The candy ceases to exist when the ego mask is destroyed entirely. Without an ego mask, Maya cannot elicit emotion from you regardless of circumstance. It is our emotional matrix, tied into the dualistic world, that gives Maya power over us and through which we feed her. She requires energy to weave the illusion of a dualistic world and she is dependent on the majority of the world's people remaining entranced and tied into it in order to keep the game afoot.

"Maya rolls up her sleeves for the self righteous ones; indignation is one of her very favorite treats."

It is from the limited view of the ego mask that we deign to delineate better or worse outcomes; that we divide people into enemies and friends. Even beyond our likes and dislikes; beyond the conceptual aspects of our mask, there are more subtle emotional levels that cannot be seen until they're brought to the surface.

When you're on a real introspective journey, or if you are practicing self-enquiry correctly, these levels *will* eventually be brought to the surface for you to deal with. In practicing self-enquiry you are constantly asking yourself, *who is it that is experiencing these thoughts in this moment? What is the nature of this "I" around which my identity revolves?* As you continue to question the basis of your internal dialogue, more and more layers of mental and emotional debris will come up for you to witness and release.

When you've dealt with all of your thousands of emotional hang ups; when you've broken through all of your conceptual retardation, that's when the ego mask will finally crumble to pieces. Where there was once reaction and emotion triggered by life's ups and downs, there will be only a peaceful abiding in nondual consciousness when the ego mask is destroyed.

The good news is that Maya is a figment of your imagination. She is your greatest foe and captor and you created her. She is your entrainment into collective consciousness and the keeper of your duality. Once you've defined yourself and prepared your mask properly, Maya is set up to play the part of the rest of the universe. Her game is duality and she is, hands down, the master. She is crafty as crafty can be and her treachery is nearly undetectable, but not completely and not forever. Her treachery cannot withstand prolonged and unwavering scrutiny should you chose to hunt her down, eliminate your ego mask and break free from her charade.

For every aspect of your ego that you perfect and polish, Maya will eventually give you a trashing with her stick. You will reformulate your ego and piece your mask together time after time and Maya will smash you again and again until one day, you start to intuit that you're playing a rather twisted game. You'll hear Maya snickering in the background as you trip over a crack in the sidewalk during your office break, holding your mask up with one hand and a frappuccino latte in the other. You'll spill your latte over your head and mask while simultaneously bowling over a fat lady in a pink mumu. You won't have time to apologize or even laugh because the lady is now threatening to sue, but instead of suing, she simply gets you fired from your job because it turns out she's the bosses daughter. This is just a humorous example. When Maya actually comes at you with her stick it might not seem so funny. The beat downs come in an endless variety and they are hand tailored based on the configurations of your ego mask.

Maya enjoys both sides of the game though. Before she can beat you down, Maya will help you build your ego mask and nurture your specialness with the hand of a meticulous artist. She will grant you beautiful things, an attractive body, a beautiful mate, ample finances, cars, houses, tropical vacations, special skills; you name it, she might let you have it. Even as she is building you up and smiling sweetly at you though; even as she is applying shiny, glittery gold to your mask, she already has one eye on how she's going to tear you down. Maya could be compared to a deranged and psychotic voodoo priestess who creates little straw dolls and breathes them into life only to revel in their screams as she pulls them apart. Little straw dolls are extremely vulnerable until they realize their fundamentally indestructible core. This is how Maya operates. This is how she keeps you tied into the game. She wants you to be pushing and pulling on the world of duality. She needs you to be tied into the outcomes of your worldly life in order to maintain her control over you.

Perhaps Maya will make you a professional athlete only to involve you in a sex scandal and eventually blow out your knee. Perhaps you'll become a multimillionaire, only to go bankrupt and end up living under the Santa Monica pier, having alienated everyone you know. How about being a supermodel whose face becomes disfigured in a fire? These are the kinds of games that Maya likes to play. She will take you up and down on her roller coaster; sometimes slowly and then at breakneck speeds, until you get wise and go running out of the amusement park entirely, screaming like a little girl all the way to the gateless gate.

When you get sick of playing the game you will go home to your true nature: nondual consciousness. You will find your true nature by frantically peeling away all of the stifling layers of mind stuff that you, your culture, the world; that Maya have caked onto you and that you have embraced and held up as your ego mask. Maya will still come a knocking on your door after your mask breaks, but you'll tell her she is not invited in. She'll try to win you back again and again and offer to repair your mask with special gifts: a new job, a better car, the perfect relationship or whatever. You might go ahead and take her gifts if you like, but you'll never again take them to heart. In your heart you'll have had enough. In your heart you'll be dead to the world, and for the first time, fully alive to the reality of nondual consciousness. One day the game will become too unbelievable and you will have no choice but to go beyond it whatever the cost. You will be like Humpty Dumpty trying to balance on the wall of life, but you will never understand Absolute Reality until either you fall and get cracked, or you surrender your shell voluntarily. Though the process may initially be quite unpleasant, you'll be relieved when your ego shell is cracked and you realize that the entire universe is made out of the yolk of consciousness (by the way if I'm ever in another music band I'm going to name it Yolk of Consciousness.)

Maya loves building us up and then beating us down. She is the ultimate sadomasochist. She enjoys both inflicting and receiving the pain and humiliation of human existence. It is what keeps the illusion of her reality alive. Maya is a naughty girl and she is also quite possessive. Though she loves to humiliate you, she doesn't really want you to escape her madness entirely. She would rather you kept frantically dangling from the tree, using all of your energy to continually rebuild your mask so she can continue to play her game and use her stick to smash you time and again.

Chapter Three

Custer's Last Stand

I AM

Everything is consciousness;
nothing can change this truth for me now.
Though I had strayed from the heart,
I came back to the center resolutely,
to surrender the ego
and be reborn as I Am.
I take the dregs of this mask
quick as I can to love's truth fire.
I am the flame itself
illuminating the shadows of this dream.
Flames leap higher
for every layer that is consumed;
flames dancing in ecstasy,
burning everything unreal.

It was late June and my wife's cousin was coming out for a visit; an unusually *long* visit. What timing. I had just spent the last year undergoing the biggest upheaval of my life to date. The details aren't really important as Maya's mad house appears differently for each person. But in my definitive bid for escape, I'd found out that the finality of ego death is unmistakable. I'd just emerged from a brutal, to the death cage match with Maya. In the end I realized I had to decimate my own ego—to commit ego mask harakiri—in order to completely transcend the game and escape from the trance of Maya's macabre illusion. I had finally emerged from the fray victorious but tired and slightly irritable, and now my wife's egomaniacal cousin was coming to stay with us for ten days.

I didn't know enough to protest or be frightened at the time. If I had known what I was in for I would have had my wife Christina call cousin Brittany and tell her that we had unfortunately come down with "mad pig spongy brain disease" or some such thing. It appeared that even though I had vanquished her and sent her packing, Maya still had some special parting gifts for me. Good for her, crafty old girl that she is; keeping me on my toes and whatnot.

Brittany continually attempted to make conversation with me at the start of her visit, but nearly everything that came out of her mouth seemed inane, like some kind of foreign language. Every other utterance that escaped her lips was an "I" statement that she would blurt out, expecting some agreement or affirmation from whomever was within earshot. She was like an energy vampire trying to fortify her dream character by sucking people's attention. She was all but incomprehensible to me at the time. If she had been anyone else, anyone not related to Christina, I simply would have remained silent. Most of the conversation she initiated had no purpose other than to bolster her ego mask.

In between telling us about her latest adventures and all the things she wanted to do while she was in town, her conversation remained squarely focused on her likes and dislikes. Conversations went something like this:

"I like this but I don't like that," Brittany would say.

"Oh," I would reply.

"This is good and this is bad,"

"Uh huh," I would say.

"I want this but I don't want that,"

"Um, that's nice," I would reply.

Listening to her talk was not preferable for me as I had recently become accustomed to a large degree of silence in my life. Try as I might to blend her into my newly acquired, mostly unimpeded nondual experience; she kept materializing and projecting herself out of it. She was like a tenacious magician continuously performing slight variations of a horrific magic trick. It was a good practice in self-enquiry. Having to put up with Brittany allowed me to see that there was still enough of me left to be slightly uncomfortable in certain situations and around certain people. There was still significant work left for me to do. In retrospect I understand fully that my discomfort during her visit had everything to do with my own remaining ego debris.

After picking Brittany up from the airport we stopped by the grocery store to grab a few things. I, being aware of Brittany's gluten free diet, told her that she might want to pick out her own bread for meals which she did. We established that tofu tacos would be agreeable for dinner as long as we used corn tortillas, that eggs were fine for breakfast and I asked her if tuna melts would be suitable for lunch the next day.

"Nooo…" Brittany sort of whined. "I don't really like tuna. Let's think of something else, k?" she said, handing her gluten free bread to Christina to pay for.

"Sure thing," I replied.

That evening, Christina, Brittany and I were sitting around the dining room table eating dinner when a pop song came on the radio that Brittany didn't approve of. The lyrics said something like, *"What if God were just an idiot like us? Just a fumbling, bumbling idiot like us?"*

"Ugh!" Brittany made a disgusted noise. "I can't believe they allow this trash to be played on the radio. Somebody ought to do something about this kind of thing."

Brittany, you see, was a Fundamentalist Christian and she was disgusted that her idea of reality was being made fun of by a modern pop song. Brittany was 27 years old and still living with her parents in Los Angeles. She had hopped around to several different colleges after high school, only to return home after not being able to figure out what she really wanted to do career wise. She had tried to move out of her parent's house once, but couldn't afford rent in L.A. so instead she moved to Beijing where she taught English for a year. After losing her job in Beijing, Brittany came back to L.A. and moved in at first with her grandma, and then back in with her parents. Things hadn't quite worked out at Grandma's house because Brittany was routinely ousted from her spare bedroom by a visiting aunt which was unacceptable. After all, she had been helping Grandma clean the house so she should have seniority when it came to who got the room right? Not really. Brittany also moved out of Grandma's house because there were too many chores to do and Grandma was just too finicky about those kinds of things.

Prior to the Beijing gig, Brittany had spent a few months in Belize saving the sea manatees, paid for of course by her parents. Prior to Belize and Beijing, Brittany had enjoyed shaking things up during her college years by bringing home "questionable" boyfriends to freak out her Fundamentalist Christian parents. Brittany seemed to truly enjoy the shock value that her boyfriends had on her family more than she really liked the poor lads themselves. She was using unfortunate unsuspecting guys to bolster her identity as a rebel and a liberal. She was about 5 foot 2, with short bobbed hair, not unattractive, around 40 pounds overweight and was a stickler for her gluten free diet which she used as a means of attempting to disguise her obvious food-centricity. Brittany was what can only be described as a rock hard ego mask with pseudo non conformist, Fundamentalist Christian, gluten free markings.

While arranging her trip with my wife Christina, Cousin Brittany informed us that she would prefer to spend the better part of her 10 day visit with us. My wife Christina had intuitively and wisely attempted to pawn her off on her parents, Brittany's aunt and uncle, for at least half of the visit, but Brittany wasn't having it. Christina's mom Lydia was the aunt that had routinely displaced her when she stayed at Grandma's house in California, not to mention Brittany said, "Lydia can be annoying after awhile."

Christina knew full well that mixing someone like Cousin Brittany with someone who had just emerged from the depths of despair: a final battle with Maya, bloodied, beheaded and not altogether "sane" could be risky. I still wasn't completely stable and I couldn't be held liable if I were unable to keep up a pleasant, socially acceptable facade. Nondual consciousness had taken over the majority of my day to day awareness, but there were still pockets of emotional crap coming up from my innermost depths to the surface from time to time. Christina however, was a very agreeable and accommodating person who had been friends with Brittany since she was a child. So here we were. It had all the makings of an unbelievable sitcom called: *Damn it Maya, You Just Won't Quit!*

At first, I noticed myself becoming a bit annoyed at Brittany's presence in my dream. I say my dream because the landscape of my conscious experience had become quite dreamlike at that time, just as my dreams had become more lifelike. The division between waking reality and dream life had become very thin in my experience. I no longer became truly annoyed or angry like I used to get as a real person, but the just *kind of* annoyed that a dream character would get, having to put up with a very boisterous, raucous, uncouth character in his dream. I had just started getting accustomed to the spacious view that lay on the other side of my ego mask. The experience was one of nearly continual peace and contentment, but somehow people with very strong egos seemed to be able to throw what I could only describe as static onto my newly expanded and spacious experience. I knew what had happened to me: ego dissolution, but it seemed that there were still some lingering traces of personal selfhood, enough to feel discomfort around very thick egos if I was forced to be in near proximity to them for any amount of time.

The day after her arrival, I offered to take Brittany to the golf course driving range with me. We were going to Christina's parent's house on the coast for the weekend and I would be playing a round of golf with my father in law Greg and some of his friends. I decided to hit the driving range preemptively so as not to embarrass myself too badly during the golf game. I asked Brittany along in order to show her some of downtown and to get her out of Christina's hair for the day. Christina was working from home and I was just a struggling writer with time on my hands.

> "I knew what had happened to me: ego dissolution, but it seemed that there were still some lingering traces of personal selfhood..."

On our way to the golf course, Brittany sang along with every song on the radio that she knew the lyrics to, even inventing lyrics where she didn't know the actual ones. She sang in an overly cheesed up dramatic pop star voice that sounded to me like a cat trying to crawl up a chalk board. I gritted my teeth and drove on, attempting all the while to maintain my practice of self-enquiry. *Who is it that is listening to Brittany pop star anyways?* I asked myself. *Is there any fundamental difference between the modulated shrieking coming from her mouth and the sound of water trickling nicely through a Zen garden stream?*

At the driving range, I spent about 45 minutes teaching Brittany how to hit golf balls. The lesson was less than successful as she had a hard time following instructions and her physique didn't exactly lend itself to the game. It was difficult for her to rotate her large shoulders past her breasts or to get any decent rotation in her wide hips. Despite her inability to hit a single ball straight though, Brittany declared that she'd like to take up golfing and start playing some courses soon. We quit when her shoulders got tired and I'd finished hitting my bucket of balls. I asked her if it'd be o.k. if we stopped by the bank on the way home as I had to take care of a couple of financial transactions.

"Um...O.K., but make it fast," she said, "I'm tired and getting hungry. I think my blood sugar is low."

"O.K., I'll make it quick," I replied, and attempted to manufacture the cheery feelings of compassion and unconditional love I had read about so many times in the Buddhist teachings. I came up short. I knew that trying to manufacture something more wasn't the answer. What I needed to do was to continue my self-enquiry in order to get rid of any last bits of myself that wanted to kick Brittany out of the car and speed off, finger in the air. I immediately switched my focus back onto myself to see where the irritation was arising from. Because most of my time was spent in a comfortable thought free, nondual state, being around Brittany felt a bit like having a splinter in my foot. I didn't dislike her, but her presence in my dream was like a repugnant smell that I couldn't get used to and that I couldn't get away from. It was the familiar and offensive smell of human ego and unhappily for me, my olfactory senses had become hyper sensitive.

At the end of the day we headed off to the coast to Christina's parent's house. Traffic was better than usual and we spent the trip listening to the album collection on my mp3 player. I purposely tried to pick albums and songs that Brittany would not know the words too, not out of malice, but because it made my dream a bit less unpleasant in those moments; just a preference you see. I was trying to avoid any sort of psychosomatic hearing loss that might be induced by prolonged exposure to her singing. Several times throughout the drive I had to disguise my snickering as coughing as Brittany valiantly made up lyrics to songs she didn't really know and mumbled them the best she could, under her breath to the tune.

We arrived at the coast a couple of hours later and I emerged gratefully from the car, ready to shoot the breeze with my father in law, and to let Brittany direct her attention toward Christina, Lydia and her new environment. We retired to the kitchen where beers were opened and drinks were made for the ladies. There was a loaf of brown rice bread on the counter and a bag of gluten free cookies. Lydia had thoughtfully prepared for Brittany's stay.

After dinner we played a board game called "Apples and Oranges," where one person drew a card with a description and each of the other players had to put down a card with a noun that best matched the description. This had never been a particularly enjoyable game for me because rather than spontaneously and objectively picking the best or most apropos answer, most players were prone to try and pick the answer that their favorite person at the table had put down. It became more a game of knowing whose answer was whose than it was of picking the most worthwhile response. The final description card of the game was "something serious". The answers laid down in response were *the mamba*; funny, I could see that getting humor points, *potato salad*; even funnier, I might even have picked that one myself under different circumstances, *high school football*; obviously Lydia playing toward Greg's preferences, and my card which I thought should have been a no brainer slam dunk: *Custer's last stand*. High school football won. Greg had played football in high school and he knew it was Lydia's card.

"You guys are fucking kidding me," I threw my cards on the table in mock exasperation, "high school football is more serious than Custer's last stand?"

I experienced some slight irritation and yet was not surprised at the outcome. Custer's last stand seemed an apt analogy of the ego death I had just undergone and I was obviously biased to that answer. Yet to some people, maybe most people, high school football would probably be considered more important than Custer's last stand, and definitely more enjoyable than ego death. For me, General Custer was my ego. He was fighting against an enemy that he had totally miscalculated and never stood a chance against. For him it was a group of American Indians that had him vastly out numbered. For me it was my self—my own mind—Maya. He died in a violent and bloody battle. My ego did the same. Who the hell would want to annihilate themselves instead of watching high school football? It made perfect sense. Though Maya had no choice but to let me go in the end, I begrudgingly had to tip my hat to her ironic comedy where in laws and board games were concerned.

"For me, General Custer was my ego. He was fighting against an enemy that he had totally miscalculated and never stood a chance against."

The next evening after dinner, I started up a conversation about Einstein's law of conservation of energy. It seemed like a good jumping off point for an interesting conversation between people at various stages of spiritual awakening. The conversation opener was a hit. Everybody bit and chimed in their two cents as to what the law meant to them. We were having a nice, safe little intellectual discussion and then, like a moron, I upped the ante.

"O.K. so how does this apply to individuality and life and death?" I asked.

"Well it really doesn't at all," Brittany stated matter-of-factly.

"I'm going to the kitchen, anybody need anything?" asked Greg getting up from the table.

"I'm just going to finish cleaning up," Lydia said following Greg's lead.

I looked at Christina and she just gave me a shrug, a half smile and slight shake of the head that said, "Do you know how to ruin a party or what?"

For me, Einstein's law of conservation of energy is one of the cornerstones of modern spirituality. It's nothing that hasn't been said before, thousands of years earlier by every one of the great spiritual traditions. But it has been made palatable to the intellect via Einstein's law, and it is abstract enough not to challenge anyone's religious or spiritual beliefs; at least when looked at on the surface. It is something that almost everyone can wrap their head around and agree upon to a certain extent.

What does it mean in the end, that energy can neither be created nor destroyed? It is a great concept that opened my mind when I was a kid. But as a newly emerged nobody experiencing nondual consciousness, it is a description of the experience that all endeavors in the dream state—I equate the world of duality with a dream state—are ultimately futile. Looked at in another way, it is a law that states that all endeavors in the dream state and their outcomes are ultimately perfect. It is an acknowledgement that everything is absolutely One without a second, and taken a couple of steps further, that the only true reality is Absolute Consciousness itself. This isn't nihilism, but a sort of super nihilism. It is an experience brought about by a death/rebirth process and an ultimate emancipation from mental bondage. It isn't just about negation. Negation is only a process: a tool used alongside self-enquiry to arrive at a final impasse. In Sanskrit, the term *neti neti* means not this, not this. It is an exercise where you negate everything that is temporary until you are left with the only truth that exists. There *is* something on the other side of total negation and that something is Absolute Reality. The desire to achieve this outcome over that, or believe *this* is truly better than *that*, requires a false individual at the center. When the false individual at the center is demolished everything is perceived as perfect.

Enlightenment, nondual consciousness, is the end game. There aren't really stages of it, only seeming stages of not it. It can be equated to withdrawing your awareness from the characters and scenes in a movie and identifying instead, only with the background screen: the pure consciousness on which the images are only ever superimposed. Enlightenment is what happens when you finally jump off the dream cliff of illusion. You let go of your belief in the duality of the world and tumble inward only to find everything reconciled in the absolute perfection of nondual consciousness.

You begin to intuit that you cannot really die; NO THING cannot be killed. When you jettison your ego mask once and for all, consciousness continues and more clearly than ever before. Absolute Reality is what you are and what you have always been. It exists as the core of your being beyond dualistic thinking, emotions and the relative experiences that continuously divert your awareness away from truth. Absolute Reality is eternal, immeasurable and unassailable. God simply IS, unchanging and perfect, and yet the picture show of Maya still appears superimposed over Absolute Reality as a temporary fictitious play.

As you adjust into the view of nondual consciousness, Maya's picture show becomes more and more intangible and dreamlike. You still see the play going on, but you're no longer tied into the outcomes of the scenes. Ideas and thoughts will still flash through your consciousness. You might still have the occasional hope that things go this way or that. Perhaps fleeting remnants of fear thoughts may occasionally flicker through the mind looking to take root, but they can't. You'll look at them and laugh. You will begin to perceive reality as it exists in the moment. And you will no longer look at things second hand through the tiny judgmental eye slits in your ego mask.

After your ego mask gets decimated and you realize you are consciousness itself, any game plans you may have previously had go out the window. There is nobody left to do anything or plan anything really. At this point there is really no one left to care. Slight preferences might remain, but it is like dreaming about being in a playground and wondering whether you'd rather play on the jungle gym or the swing. It's just a dream and you know it. Whatever happens is for the best.

If there is any sort of over reaching pattern for the way you appear to move about through life after ego destruction, it is to bring about the best outcome possible for everyone involved as an agent of Mother Consciousness. You're awake in your dream and just kind of enjoying it. It becomes a game that you're not really playing so much as witnessing once the ego has been destroyed. You are Absolute Reality and the game of life is simply being projected all around you. There is no one left to get upset about not achieving goals or not having things go your way. You're just grooving around, kind of witnessing what your dream character is doing in the moment.

> "When you abide in nondual consciousness life flows on without much deliberation, and there's no longer even a decision making process so much as a continual acquiescing to the reality of each moment."

When other people get upset about some aspect of the dream, you might nod and sympathize with their dream plight, or more likely, you'll be so unimpressed by their imaginary problems that you will try to guide them gently, or not so gently, or not at all, to the realization that it is and always has been just a dream. More than likely that is what you'll do in some way. In the beginning you may notice that many of the people in your life begin to fall away. People that are strongly tied into the world and worldly things will no longer have much in common with you. Discussing worldly things can become quite tedious when you are awake in the dream. The conversations that you have with people that last beyond a few pleasantries will likely end up meandering into "spiritual" territory. Everything other than "truth talk" becomes like mental masturbation and it's difficult to pay much attention to it.

When you abide in nondual consciousness life flows on without much deliberation, and there's no longer even a decision making process so much as a continual acquiescing to the reality of each moment. There is no wavering back and forth because rather than making decisions, you are simply surrendering to the will of Mother Consciousness completely. Every moment is spent falling further and further into the Absolute Reality of existence. The more you surrender, the more you realize that whatever the outcome of any situation, it is perfect. There actually are no such things as outcomes anymore because you are experiencing everything in the moment, and this moment is the pinnacle of, and sum total of, all possibilities always. At a certain point, you realize that everything that is meant to be accomplished will undoubtedly be accomplished, and at the same time you realize that nothing is really happening or has ever really happened anyway. "Wake up and smell the emptiness," you'll say to people. The best part of waking up is nothing in your cup.

CHAPTER FOUR

Independence Day

SPINNING INTO FREEDOM

The shadow of my ego
disappeared in the truth I longed to find.
I fell, spinning like a whirling dervish,
out of control and out of time.
When the shadow was lifted and consciousness lay clean,
I peered around and saw only eternity.
Consciousness beckons us every moment,
"Let it go," she says. "Let it go and rest in me."
I have no choice. I go without hesitation,
driven by the siren call of Freedom!

Inward ho, into her spontaneous design;
I go full speed, and rest forever out of time.
Dying to the world,
I reach the pinnacle of silence:
emptiness poised at the Mysterious Gate,
where I no longer dream in time,
yet time goes on dreaming through me.

On our way back from the coast on Sunday, we ran into a large car accident that was blocking the highway out of town for miles. We had to turn around and back track to the coast in order to take the southern route home.

"Ughh! How long is this going to take now?" whined Brittany. "I get car sick and it's starting to get hot back here. Can you turn up the air conditioner or something?"

"Sure, I'll turn up the air conditioner," I replied, "but this trip is going to seem even longer if somebody gets to whining and complaining."

"What! I wasn't whining!" Brittany whined. "I'm just saying."

Two and a half tedious hours later we returned home and Christina and I resumed trying to keep our sanctuary happy and peaceful. Thankfully Brittany spent several of her remaining vacation days riding Christina's bicycle into town to explore. Brittany had mentioned on several occasions, in a hinting manner, that when she visited other friends, generally they would just lend her their cars. As tempting as it was to give her greater mobility to roam far away, Christina and I both knew how that would probably end up: Brittany running into something or someone with the car and forever unable to pay us back for the damage.

Brittany would return from her bicycle rides in the evenings to recount all the amazing gluten free foods she had found in the town restaurants. One day she texted excitedly about a raw, gluten free lasagna she had found at one of the vegan food carts in town. *This lasagna is amazing. The food in this town is so great! I think I could live here!*

Uh oh.

One evening after dinner, Brittany and I fell into a bit of a "spiritual" conversation.

"What kind of spiritual teaching do you follow?" asked Brittany.

"I follow the teaching of no self," I replied.

"Well what the heck does that mean?"

I knew that I was barking up the wrong tree as far as this conversation went, but I couldn't help myself. Here was this tiny space where Brittany and I might be able share a bit of reality together, so I was compelled to try.

"It means that in order to experience truth you have to go beyond your temporary ego self. The more things you hold on to; the more you scatter your energy through attachments to ideas, philosophies, people and situations, the more stuck you are in a finite, theoretical world and the further you'll be from truth."

"Well do you believe in the afterlife?" Brittany asked, seemingly not having paid attention to anything I had just said. "Where do you believe the spirit goes after death?"

Oh no. This was about to get ugly. I could already see Brittany's breathing starting to become rapid and shallow as she prepared to defend her staunch beliefs about the afterlife. Despite my best efforts to resist going down the rabbit hole, my mouth opened and this came out:

"Death doesn't exist for me anymore," I replied. "I don't recognize a difference between spirits and bodies and there is no afterlife for me. For me nothing exists except for the reality in this moment right here right now. Consciousness is eternal and it's not really divided into bodies and spirits."

"For me nothing exists except for the reality in this moment right here right now."

Brittany tensed up. I could see her wheels turning. She was wondering whether to launch into a verbal tirade defending her beliefs or to withdraw into a silent condescension where I would simply be mentally pigeonholed as a heretic and a lunatic. After a tense moment, Brittany opened up the attic of her mind and placed me squarely on a dusty shelf somewhere in between Charles Manson and Bozo the Clown. She made the wise choice.

"Um, O.K., Well I've got to go check my emails now," Brittany replied rolling her eyes.

Brittany never brought up spirituality in front of me again. For the rest of the week, Brittany spent her time lounging on the couch, riding Christina's bike into town and chatting with friends online. Our conversations were kept to the minimum formalities and I spent the majority of my time hiding in my study attempting to write. It wasn't easy to access a clear mental space while Brittany was around. I had always been able to feel people's energy and I could literally feel Brittany's presence looming in the house, like a big raucous specter. By the end of the week, to my absolute non surprise, Brittany had managed to completely ignore the one agreement she had made with Christina prior to her visit: that she would help weed the back garden in payment for her lodging.

"Oops," Brittany said to Christina on her last day at our house, "I totally didn't get to the gardening did I?"

Had I been present at that moment, Maya probably would have been whispering in my ear to grab Brittany by the nose and twist. Of course I would never do such a thing, but I imagine Maya would have made a compelling argument. Thankfully, Christina doesn't really have a mean bone in her body, but I imagine even her fist must have clenched just ever so slightly.

We had made plans to spend the weekend—Brittany's last weekend of vacation—back at the beach with Christina's parents. Her parents had a much larger house with more space for everyone to occupy themselves and their egos in. And Brittany, so we reasoned, would be less inclined to be bratty in front of her aunt and uncle. Brittany didn't really want to go back to the beach. She didn't say so at the time, but she would later tell Christina during an angry rant that, "I'm like only 20 percent a beach person and 80 percent a forest person. I really wanted to stay and explore the town and do some more hiking in the forests, but we only get to do what Michael wants to do."

During Brittany's stay, Christina and I had done everything that we could to provide Brittany with entertainment. We cooked special gluten free meals for her and provided her with free room and board. Her aunt and uncle, Christina's parents, were generous and accommodating hosts to Brittany, as they were to all their guests. And still Brittany managed only to focus on what was wrong with the situation, and the ways in which things hadn't gone exactly to her liking. I, of course, did have an inkling that Brittany didn't want to go back to the beach for a second weekend, but because she never said so, I decided I would do what was best for everyone involved. Brittany's Aunt Lydia actually wanted to spend time with the poor child, bless her soul. So on Friday, we all piled into the car and headed back to the coast. On Saturday July 3rd, Christina's parents took us out to dinner. Afterward, we planned on going down to the beach for the local fireworks show.

"Are we almost there?" asked Brittany on the way to the restaurant, "Cause I'm sick of riding in the car."

"Why don't you just ask it right?" I said.

"What do you mean?"

"You're supposed to ask 'Are we there yet?' and draw it out in a really whiney voice."

Brittany smiled as if we were playing an inside joke together.

"Arrre weeee theeeeere yehhht?" Brittany whined toward Greg who was driving, oblivious to the fact that I wasn't really kidding and that she really did come across as a whiney, discontented 8 year old most of the time.

After dinner we arrived at the fireworks show. Greg dropped off Brittany, Lydia and I to go find a place to set up chairs. There were some large open spaces with the best views at the top of a grassy hill and I suggested to Lydia and Brittany that we pick one of those large spaces up top to set up.

"No I want to sit here," Brittany said pointing to a lower spot in between two other groups of people.

"But Brittany, the view is better up there and there aren't any people around so we can all fit comfortably," I said.

Lydia just looked at me and then back at Brittany trying to decide what to do.

"I don't care. I just think we should sit here," Brittany replied. "I don't want anyone to sit in front of me and block the view."

That didn't make any sense whatsoever.

"But Brittany the grade is so steep up there that even if someone sat directly in front of us it wouldn't block the view…"
Brittany just looked at me defiantly.

"O.K., why don't you guys just sit here and Christina and I will sit up there," I said. I set up chairs for the two of them and moved the rest of the gear up the hill to a wide open space. After parking the car, both Christina and Greg came and sat next to me, about 10 feet up from where Brittany and Lydia were sitting, sandwiched in between two other groups of people.

"Why are they sitting down there?" asked Greg.

"I don't know," I replied. "Brittany just wanted to sit there."

"Ha! Ha!" Greg just laughed good naturedly. "Well good for them," he said and cracked open a couple of beers for us.

Several times throughout the show Lydia looked back and tried to talk Brittany into joining the rest of us higher up on the hill, but to no avail. As I glanced at the back of Brittany's head it seemed as if I could actually see her ego looming, like a big dark cloud, with tentacles that tenaciously tried to control everything in her immediate proximity. The fireworks came and went: a beautiful show over the ocean, and Brittany had triumphed in her obstinate stance, even getting her Aunt Lydia to sit with her for the entire show.

The next day Brittany was scheduled to fly out in the afternoon. It was July 4th, Independence Day. Christina and I had planned to leave her parents house with just ample time to get Brittany dropped off at the airport on the way home, but Brittany had other plans. When she asked Christina if they could go for a walk together that morning, the smell of Brittany's agenda was obvious to me. She had some things to say to Christina and she didn't want me around to hear. Christina looked at me questioningly as she and I had been planning to take a walk together that morning. I, sensing what was afoot, gave her a wink and waved her on. It was during that walk that Brittany revealed that she hadn't wanted to go to the beach *again* for the weekend at all, that she was really a forest person and not a beach person, that she had felt trapped all weekend long and that they only ever do what Michael wants to do. She also said that we had promised to take her to the winery and hadn't, and so we really ought to leave early to go there like we promised.

Christina and Brittany returned to the house and Christina told me about Brittany's discontentment. We decided to change our plan and arranged for Christina to take Brittany into town early and for me to stay at the beach for another day of golf with her dad. Christina and Brittany quickly packed and prepared to leave.

"Do you like cats?" Lydia asked Brittany as they were saying their goodbyes.

The question had been prompted by me and Christina's grey and white tabby Mr. Kahuna, who was running around the house trying to escape capture as usual. He would routinely notice that bags were being packed and something was going on, and try to hide every time we were getting ready to leave.

"No I really don't like cats," Brittany replied. "I'm like totally a dog person."

Everyone said their goodbyes, Christina, Brittany and Mr. Kahuna all packed into the car and they were off. Greg and I high fived each other back in the house as Lydia stood outside waving goodbye. It was Independence Day and I had learned a valuable lesson about screening house guests. I decided that in the future, I would come up with an ego to time ratio that would determine to the minute, how long guests were welcome to stay. According to my calculations, had the ratio been in effect prior to Brittany's arrival, she would have been allowed to stay exactly 37 minutes.

So what does this have to do with enlightenment anyway? Rather let me tell you what it has to do with non enlightenment. Brittany and I were brought together to illustrate very vividly how not to flow with the universe. Her ego mask is a perfect, if somewhat obvious example, of what it is that holds each of us back from unobstructed happiness. I couldn't have come up with a better imaginary character to serve as ego's poster child if I had tried. The dialogue alone was priceless.

Anytime you adamantly want things your way or no way at all, there is a major disconnect between self and other. When you are enlightened there is no self, no other, and you are then capable of abiding within the totality of a situation. By the very nature of your consciousness, you have a tendency to guide things gently and silently towards the best possible outcome for everyone involved. It is your very nature to do so as you are no longer running a strong personal agenda. Things happen, things change, circumstances come and go and you become more of a witness than someone with definite aims and strong opinions. When there is no self and no other, everything is well and everything is experienced as transpiring perfectly. Consciousness becomes the all pervading backdrop on which everything plays itself out beautifully.

"Consciousness becomes the all pervading backdrop on which everything plays itself out beautifully."

Weeks later, Christina and I were discussing Brittany's stay. The discussion had been prompted by the fact that Brittany had left with the key to my bicycle lock and had not yet mailed it back. It would eventually be one month, many text messages (including one from her Uncle Greg) and an email later that I finally got my key back. When the key finally did arrive it came complete with a Raggedy Andy thank you card.

I mentioned to Christina that I was puzzled that a 27 year old woman, without a job and living with her parents, could have such a definitive attitude and be so utterly obstinate. Christina then revealed the missing piece of the Brittany puzzle to me. It turned out that Brittany had been very popular in high school. She had been very active on the dance team and was in really great physical shape at that time. She was the "it" girl amongst the high school elite and had even been voted prom queen her senior year. That little world had been her oyster and she was still accustomed to getting everything she wanted. The picture clicked into place for me then. Brittany had reached the pinnacle of her ego development in high school and hadn't really moved a single step forward since. She had gotten stuck in the role of being the most popular cool kid around and was still putting it on, even when the audience had no context. Brittany had yet to encounter any resistance; she hadn't had any life obstacles capable of disrupting her ego mask so far. For Brittany, everything was filtered through a very particular and narrow set of criteria. She was puzzled that anyone would ever want to do something other than what she wanted. She was puzzled anytime things didn't go her way. Her ego piñata was dangling gleefully from the tree of life, dancing in the wind. But if she ever stopped to listen closely, I guarantee she would have heard the unmistakable swoosh of Maya's stick breezing just past the edge of her mask.

Reality is what remains when your ego mask has been decimated. As long as the ego is intact you will always be troubled by the idea of better and worse situations, likes and dislikes; hopes and fears. Without the hindrance of an ego mask, Absolute Reality simply is, and what is, is God. Everything is God; everything is pure absolute consciousness itself.

From this perspective, even Brittany's visit and her incessant whining were perfect. I acknowledged it as such and was therefore not nearly as dismayed as I would have been without this realization.

Granted that her presence was not my preference at the time, but the universe knows better than I do, and I know better than to think anything should be other than the way it is. In retrospect, I now know that we were brought together by Mother Consciousness to illustrate some important points. The timing was flawless and the visit generated some excellent material.

During the time Brittany was in my presence it was energetically uncomfortable for the both of us. The discomfort was purely physics. She and I were like two energies vibrating at wildly different speeds. I was incapable of strengthening, upholding or even recognizing her ego. And to me, her presence in my consciousness was simply like an unpleasant cartoon character in my dream that couldn't help but make a lot of obscene noises.

From Brittany's perspective, events and circumstances had to fall into a very particular design that pleased her in order for her to be content, namely the design of her ego. If things varied even slightly from her preferences she voiced an opinion or got upset. For Brittany, life will be very hard and eventually very unpleasant until she begins to move beyond her egocentric fortress and open up to, and accept the truth of *what is*.

For me, what is, is all there is. What is, is God. There is just ever present nondual consciousness. This consciousness is open and free. It is very simple and unmistakably eternal and infinite. Our only job is to withdraw this consciousness from the thoughts, emotions, circumstances and people that tie us into the relative dualistic world in order to experience the totality of *what is*. For me, the only times that this nondual consciousness seems to be disrupted are times when there are interactions with people, organizations or institutions that are strongly mired in the illusion of duality. Those instances simply feel uncomfortable and somewhat alien, like a cloud palpably blocking the sun. It feels alien to me because these people, organizations or institutions are projecting strong paradigms of duality with their ego/minds that tentatively cover what I normally experience as one unified whole. At those times, simply realizing that my awareness has been pulled outward by collective consciousness and withdrawing my awareness out of the disturbance and back into my heart center[4] usually suffices to disperse the uncomfortable feeling, and return me to the unobstructed flow of nondual consciousness. That is a basic summary of the entire practice. Self-enquiry is continually withdrawing your conscious awareness from the periphery of the world and worldly thoughts and into the absolute center. At first this practice requires the faith that Mother Consciousness—God—is attending perfectly to the entire universe and does not require your worry or mental chatter in order to do her job correctly.

"Self-enquiry is continually withdrawing your conscious awareness from the periphery of the world and worldly thoughts and into the absolute center."

If you want to gauge how far you've gone along the path of no self ask yourself this: when was the last time you became really upset? When was the last time you became utterly disappointed or angry at someone or some circumstance? Are there things, people or situations that you truly hate? What are you still afraid of? How deep do those fears run? How much doubt do you have? Are you worried that you are not on the right path? Are you distraught because you're not sure which direction to go in? Do you think you can get it wrong? How many times per minute and per hour are you bouncing worry thoughts off of other people and situations? The honest answers to these questions will show you where you stand. All doubts will dissipate to the extent that you get beyond your ego mask and identify fully with nondual consciousness: the realization of the perfection of Absolute Reality.

---

[4]The "heart center" is a metaphor that is used frequently in the teachings of Ramana Maharshi. It describes the still space of nondual consciousness that is reached when one successfully disengages their awareness from the periphery of ego/mind activity.

Once you extricate yourself from the confines of the ego mask, life becomes really quite pleasant. All that "enlightenment" really means is an unimpeded experience of nondual consciousness. It isn't relatively exciting and beings don't generally materialize from nirvana to throw flowers at your feet or place garlands around your neck. Being awake however is very fluid, natural and open; like always being at home wherever you are.

CHAPTER FIVE

Underneath the Mask

ZERO STATE

I rest in consciousness.
Every breath draws me deeper
into light.
Every moment I follow silence
to the zero state.
From silence I behold the beauty
and absurdity of this world.
From silence I rectify
the bitter-sweet song of human life.
I dissolve all mental cages
and renounce all hope and fear.
From silence I expand
from a single point
into the absolute universal truth.
Consciousness lights the world on fire here:
from this silence
that dismantles you and I.

When the ego has been pulverized and consciousness has been unmasked, there may seem to be some residual things to work out: like how do you interact with other people? Is it still possible to make small talk? Is there a well defined career path for "enlightened folks"? In my experience, during the period that I was undergoing ego pulverization and total unmasking, I was thankfully set apart from society for awhile. My wife and I had just moved to a new town where we didn't know anyone. I was in between jobs and trying my hand at writing. It was nearly a year long transition during which I underwent a complete unraveling of myself. All of my ideas, emotions, tendencies, negative and positive attributes, relationships past and present; everything that comprised my identity as an individual was brought forth, examined and then surrendered. Some of these emotions and tendencies were exacerbated and boiled to the surface violently as I increased the intensity of my self enquiry. But as they came up, I remained like a samurai cutting through every emotional tendency and energetic tendril that emanated from my mind and tied me into the dualistic world of illusion. What remained in the aftermath was consciousness itself, unfettered, silently witnessing the flow of life.

I had lost the impetus that had tied me into the movie as a particular character and became more like the light shining through the projector, without which the movie could never be projected. The process was one of withdrawing consciousness and energy out of the scenes and just allowing the projection of life to take place as it would, identifying instead with the all pervading light that comprised the whole show. The scenes were still there, the play was still going on, but I was tracing back everything I perceived with my senses until my awareness remained squarely where external phenomenon converged with pure consciousness itself. I fell back in upon myself like a supernova and found that at the center, there was only this one undifferentiated conscious awareness. There at the center, everything was God and there was no longer anything left for me to desire or achieve as an individual.

Although the experience continues to clarify and stabilize itself, and I still occasionally encounter some residual ego debris, there is a certainty that this nondual consciousness cannot really be covered up again to any real extent. My character is pretty funny and still has some really good lines to deliver no doubt, but I can never again forget that what appears to be life is relatively just an act. The finality of what occurred to me during that transitional year is unmistakable, and still, the open ended nature of this process is undeniable.

The dichotomy of enlightened versus unenlightened is a paradox like all things that can be spoken of. The reality however, is only one. When I say that enlightenment is both final and open ended at the same time, I simply mean that there is a critical jumping off point that is very clear. The destruction of the ego mask is an ending and a beginning, like all moments in time, but one that is particularly salient if ever anything was. You could say that at this point, I consider myself to have undergone a rather final unmasking. Now even if I wanted to, it would be exceedingly difficult to try to put on, or create any new mask additions with which I could separate myself from the dualistic world falsely, or with which I would attempt to impose a particular agenda upon the world. I register and acknowledge people, things and situations, but am mostly focused on the consciousness that comprises these things: the center to which all things return. The very impetus for trying to put on a mask—ultimately the fear of death, the fear of eternity, or the fear of non-being—is simply no longer present for me. I am experiencing myself as reality itself and that reality appears to have a momentum of its own, relatively speaking. Our duty if there is such a thing; is only to get ourselves out of the way enough to let the master playwright work. The script is written and we are always, every one of us, whether it seems like it or not, experiencing the proper circumstances in life. It's not really a question of what lines you will utter or what actions you will take in a particular scene, it's only a question of the spirit with which you will deliver, based on the depth of consciousness you are experiencing in the moment.

This brings us to the point of free will versus destiny. Free will versus destiny is, like all other dichotomies, a false division. This false division can only be made if you believe in the existence of a separate finite self who is autonomously calling his or her own shots. It certainly appears as if this is the case, but only because the ego mask is so limited and shortsighted, and Maya is such a master of deception. If consciousness is all that exists and we are that, there is necessarily something comprehensive, beyond our seemingly finite selves that is putting on the entire show. That something is what I refer to as Mother Consciousness.

"...the more you get toward the nondual spectrum of consciousness, the funnier even tragedy begins to appear."

Again, I use Absolute Reality, God and Mother Consciousness interchangeably. Similarly, Maya could be equated with Satan for those of Christian faith. The reality is that God/Mother Consciousness is the only truth. Maya and Satan are the illusions. They are the veil that distorts the perfection of what we are and have always been. Our job is simply to take back the power we have granted these illusions in order to experience the one Absolute Reality. We take back the power we have granted to Maya/Satan by releasing and transcending the negative emotions and judgments that serve to reinforce the veil of dualism. Again the most direct way that I know of to do this is through self enquiry, and relatively speaking, it takes hard work and time.

When the veil is utterly torn asunder, God remains as the only experience, and the only truth that exists. Unfortunately it's not enough to simply understand this conceptually, that is only the start. I've heard some Advaita teachers telling their students that indeed there is no practice to do because they have never existed as individuals in the first place. While this might be the truth ultimately, it can be a bit of a useless teaching for people who really do feel, with every fiber of their being, that their problems are real, that their bodies are real and that the world is real. The false conditioning that comprises one's ego mask has been built up over a long, long time and so, relatively speaking, undoing that conditioning will necessarily take some effort. Maya generally won't just pack up and leave because you once muster up the courage to tell her you don't believe in her. No, she's much more persistent than that. Maya is the archetype of all disease; she is the epitome of negativity. Maya is original sin itself and taking back all your power and emotion from her will therefore take time for most people. Not everyone can explode into a mystical ball of light just by once acknowledging God as the only reality.

Mother Consciousness runs the entire show, and yet she allows Maya to try and make us believe that it is us as individual egos who are dictating the play. It is the crux of the game of life. Maya sets up the show by helping us to create our ego mask and then playing the part of the rest of the seemingly separate universe. Mother Consciousness simply comprises the characters and scenes and imbues them with the light that allows them to dance upon the screen in an ephemeral play. Life is going to be funny and life is going to be tragic. But the more you get toward the nondual spectrum of consciousness, the funnier even tragedy begins to appear. It's not that Mother Consciousness is purposely morose or twisted; it's just that she is the final punch line in the ultimate cosmic joke, and the joke has always been our separate, finite existence. Everything we say, every time we open our mouths has a tint of humor to it. The joke is that we are illusory characters speaking to other illusory characters in a dream. More than that, we are the consciousness that comprises the entirety of the dream itself.

The play of life as we know it cannot exist without dialogue. Dialogue is one of the most obvious arenas in which people examine and feel out each others ego masks thereby allowing them to play out their appointed roles. In a world where everyone was enlightened I imagine language would not be necessary. Silence would be the milieu wherein everything transpired perfectly amongst people who were knowingly unified into an integrated whole. As it is, we fashion words as a means of upholding our version of reality and then bandy them about, jousting and play fighting with other egos. Strong egos lend themselves to strong words and arguments. Nondual consciousness lends itself to silence; or at least, softer, funnier words. It seems that the lines that Mother Consciousness is feeding me these days don't particularly lend themselves to drama or soap operas. I happen to be more of a comedy guy. For the most part, I can't take anything seriously anymore. Everything has become rather laughable in fact. Unless I'm talking about "spiritual" stuff, nearly every other utterance out of my mouth is a joke. When you see things clearly, the relative world is necessarily funny because duality is the ultimate yuk-yuk. It's a beautiful joke mind you, an elegant charade as I call it, and humor along with poetry seem to be the most apropos ways I've found to point it out.

The plain fact of the matter is that the appearance of reality is just an illusion. Time, space, consciousness and reality are all one undifferentiated motionless light. What I used to consider myself: the body/mind phenomena: is now like a translucent image floating in this light. It flickers onto the screen of the world, but most definitely is not apart from the light in any way. Reality, in truth, remains shining and unchanging right where it has always been. The light is the only truth; oneness is the only truth. The actors are ephemeral images; try as they might to assert their independence from the light it can never be done.

The only things that perpetuate our illusion of separation are the thoughts and emotions that comprise our ego masks. Those repetitive thoughts and emotions act like floatation devices that pull us out of the depths of inner consciousness and onto the surface of the dualistic world. The ego mask is only a conglomeration of thoughts and emotions that have been congealed into the appearance of a separate entity over time. That separate entity is like a large raft for some people, for others it is a huge cruise ship that keeps their awareness firmly on the illusory surface of life.

Like all creations, the ego mask must one day dissipate. For some, the ego mask happens to get destroyed while the body is still alive and being projected into the world. This is what is generally termed enlightenment. It is the experience of nondual consciousness that is reached when your ship is destroyed and your awareness merges into the depths of nondual consciousness, where everything is experienced as Absolute Reality. The ship may still appear to exist to other people on the surface, but the appearance is just an illusion as personal consciousness has merged into the light of Absolute Reality. I use the term "light" because it is the most accurate for me. Other people describe this reality as "emptiness" or "void", but no term can adequately capture the nature of Absolute Reality which is why I prefer to use several terms interchangeably.

The ego mask will begin to unravel when you get the impetus to look deeply into your thoughts and your identity. Who are you really? You have to lock onto this enquiry and ride it all the way to the final dissolution of your finite self. Again, it can be difficult to generate enough energy to really blow away your own ego when life circumstances are going relatively peachy keen. When you're trying to blow up a huge ship, it's harder to do it with hugs and kisses or sedative-like spiritual crap than it is to do with the dynamite of volatile disconsolation. There is, in general, always some deep gnawing dissatisfaction with your perceived reality that puts the process into overdrive. It is the type of gnawing dissatisfaction that can have you up at 3 a.m., wild eyed and yelling at God to either give you truth or give you death.

There is a part of you that knows full well that all of the constructs that you have tied yourself into and used to define yourself are lies. When that part of you becomes loud enough and insistent enough, you will begin to question yourself mercilessly to the point of ego destruction. Until that time you will reside in your old comfortable thought patterns. If those thought patterns start to get old and weary you might replace them with newer and shinier thought patterns, but newer and shinier thought patterns will only ever change the markings on your mask and serve to repair your ship. The power of positive thinking I'm sorry to say, is no better than the power of negative thinking. On the one side, a positive mask looks all shiny and pretty. On the flip side, a negative mask looks ugly and mean. To me, absolutely no mask is the most beautiful vision to be had.

What you need if you're really serious about going all the way with ego dissolution, is a gnawing dissatisfaction with the entire charade that eventually turns into a full blown quest for freedom, live or die. Very few people want this kind of absolute truth. Most are only looking to create and perpetuate an ever more comfortable charade. Most people are simply seeking a nice smooth voyage on their ego's luxury cruise line.

When the time is ripe though, when you do finally begin to tear away at your mask with utter abandon, it would be best to be on holiday somewhere far away from other people. It would be ideal to be in the woods or somewhere in nature; somewhere where yelling and screaming can't be heard and the wild look in your eyes won't be frightening to the neighbors. While you are undergoing final ego unmasking, other people in your life may not understand what is happening to you. They may even become uncomfortable and try to keep you in a mask; in a role that is acceptable to them. The reason for this is simple: within our own ego constructs we have an idea of how other people should behave in relationship to us and to society. We have certain expectations of how others close to us should be playing out their appointed roles, and for most people, the desirability or even the

"Most are only looking to create and perpetuate an ever more comfortable charade."

option of breaking free from one's roles remains unknown. From the view point of a solid ego mask, watching someone you know break free from the confines of his or her ego mask—from the confines of society and the world of duality—can be upsetting.

When my wife and I moved to a new city, she found gainful employment almost immediately. I on the other hand was having a difficult time finding a suitable work situation and consequently, decided to roll with it and try my hand at what I had always wanted to do: writing. All of this was taking place while I was undergoing a final ego dissolution which made it all the more unlikely that I could just run out and find any old job at that moment. Who would want to hire a lunatic anyway? In the throes of this particular personal meltdown, I was about as stable as a manic depressive cat with psychotic tendencies. One of the only people that we were in frequent contact with during that time, Christina's father, became for a short while, uncomfortable with my apparent lack of ambition and motivation.

Greg had held a very successful middle management position in a very prominent software company until his recent retirement. He had accrued the nice house, the bonuses, the accolades and prestige of a well orchestrated career, and enough money for him and Lydia to ride out the rest of their years comfortably: the American dream. Greg told me in no uncertain terms during those days that Christina and I were in charge of earning our own money. He told us pointedly that he planned on spending every dime of his hard earned wealth before he died, and given my lack of gainful employment, he might have believed I had an agenda of trying to lean on him financially. I wasn't fitting the mold of what a man in society should be: hard working, industrious, ambitious; a solid take the bull by the horns kind of guy and ultimately, very financially successful.

I couldn't have fit those standards anymore if I had wanted to. Not in the conventional sense at least. The truth is that someone who is pursuing nondual consciousness through ego annihilation is anything but a slouch. What Greg couldn't see was that the amount of energy it was taking me to destroy the last strongholds of my ego mask was tremendous. What was left, what he was looking at in the aftermath, was something completely different than what he had remembered me to be. I was emptier now. I was pure choice-less awareness. My mask was gone and I no longer had the impetus to initiate anything as an individual. I could only wait as a witness for Mother Consciousness to carry me wherever she would. I was "doing by non-doing" as the Taoists would say. And from the outside I'm sure it looked like I really was doing nothing. I wasn't looking for sympathy or even understanding though. I simply trusted Mother Consciousness to lead me to whatever it was that she would have me do entirely, and in her own time. For me it didn't even really matter what was happening or what things looked like on the surface. My ship still appeared to be there, but my awareness was happily sunk into the depths of nondual consciousness.

My ego unmasking was understandably a bit uncomfortable for him to witness. He believed that he had co-created his wealth and that any individual given enough hard work could do, should do the same. A man in our society should be out kicking ass and taking names. I should have been a man with a righteous plan, setting forth to bend the universe to my will. Truthfully, if that is what Mother Consciousness had intended for me, I would have been all suits and neck ties. I would have been all cheesy jokes and business calls, driving a BMW with a Bluetooth welded directly into my ear. But it wasn't a time for things like that and that wasn't the path for me. I was bent and broken, peering into the last bits of my sanity. All I could do was go inward and wait in complete trust for Mother Consciousness to guide me faithfully, in the reality of this one never ending moment.

CHAPTER SIX

Mo' Money

IMAGINE TRUTH

Imagine that every cubic inch of space
is comprised of total consciousness,
and no matter what you do
or where you go,
you can never really fail.
Imagine that the only choice
we have in every moment
is whether to increase or decrease
the illusion of separation.

One of the most interesting and palpable challenges of living in this big charade is money. As a "spiritual person" in the world how should you go about making money? The answer to this question is the same as the answer to solving any problem in the relative world. You have to quit focusing on the problem entirely. Don't look at money as a problem. Don't feed the dichotomy of wealth versus poverty with emotion. Step back from the entire situation and listen to Mother Consciousness carefully. She will speak to you and lead you in the appropriate direction and into the appropriate situation. So what if you are meant to be poor for awhile? It won't matter if your consciousness is fully merged in reality. What matters is bringing the totality of your consciousness to bear on whichever part of you believes something can go wrong.

Enlightenment is about losing your person-hood entirely. What happens after that, well...various people in Advaita Vedanta have described it as being like a fan that has had the plug pulled out: the blades just continue to turn for awhile (not a very good business strategy I'm afraid). Actually, an enlightened person is something much more dynamic than a fan with the plug pulled out. Rather, an enlightened person has transcended his or her fan-ness and become more like the electricity that powers the fan: pure energy itself. The energy may or may not be channeled back into the fan depending on the designs of Mother Consciousness. When Maya has been utterly defeated, Mother Consciousness steps in and the paradigm shifts entirely.

Mother Consciousness and Maya are seemingly two completely different paradigms. But in reality, Mother Consciousness simply encompasses and comprises the duality of Maya. Consciousness just is, and to quote a well known movie, "stupid is what stupid does," or something like that. Consciousness finds its level and the world continues to manifest and spin around it. Stupidity finds its level and gets mired into the world of illusion accordingly. As I'm writing this, I have no idea if this endeavor will ever provide me with any income.

I only know that I was meant to write this book. Either I will make enough money to survive in this world in the future or I won't. To be perfectly honest, at this point I'm not sure if existing in this world is any better than not existing in it. I don't believe I recognize the difference anymore. What I do know for certain is that everything is working out exactly as it should, and that all is well.

Right now I have a roof over my head, a full belly and a cup of coffee. This moment is all that exists. In this moment writing seems to be what's going on so here I am. Does Mother Consciousness want this book to be in your hands? Will she guide me to be able to make enough money to afford food and clothes? Tune in next week for the answer to these questions. But seriously, mostly such thoughts don't occur to me anymore as I'm always in the present moment these days.

Consciousness just continually exists as open and free. This body will follow it wherever it leads, which is in reality, nowhere and everywhere. There is no real coming and going when abiding in nondual consciousness. Worry thoughts may still occasionally pop up, but they are immediately witnessed and then just float away. Any worry thoughts that I do have these days seem to actually be the worries of other people that I'm just receiving through the airwaves on radio station MAYA 101.1. Worries, like all thoughts, are rather foreign to nondual consciousness. When they do arise they seem to be like airy, ephemeral bubbles only lightly superimposed over consciousness itself. Even as they are drifting tenuously across the surface of the sea of consciousness, they are dissipating because I no longer breathe any life into them.

There may be the capacity and ability to utilize thoughts and words to elucidate the experience of nondual consciousness, but that is about it. Without thoughts there are no problems. Without problems, all is well and everything is unfolding as it should. The overall feeling is that everything is O.K. and that Mother Consciousness is benevolent, fair and absolutely abundant. Consciousness is pure abundance itself. It is the greatest treasure that exists and it comprises absolutely everything. We are absolute consciousness itself so what could really be left to want? This is the solution to money problems and every other type of problem that appears to exist in the relative world: go beyond it. Maintain nondual consciousness and you cannot help but find the appropriate circumstances.

In reality, abundance need not be generated or manifested. It just needs to be recognized as being really all there is. It's everything else that is the lie. Poverty, starvation, economic disaster and disease are all a joke. All these things are total lies because death itself is a lie. I know this can be hard to swallow. Stop for a minute and see how your mind is reacting to these statements. These are harsh statements to make but this isn't a book on how to soothe the ego. It is a book on how to destroy it.

Fear is the crux of Maya's game. It's the pretense of lack and limitation that has like 99.9% of the world running around frantically trying to make something happen; pushing and pulling on the world. It's as if we're bathing in an endless sea of milk and honey; we're actually made out of this milk and honey ourselves, and still Maya is sitting there successfully convincing us there's a shortage of milk and honey. When you realize consciousness as all there is, you can no longer die and you experience life as abundance itself. The trees are your treasure, the sidewalk is your foundation, the sky is your lover and you are the unlimited nondual consciousness holding it all together; creating it all. That tends to solve financial worries quite well. All problems are transcended because there is no individual left to recognize any such thing as a problem.

I know this can feel tricky. I know it's easy to say these things when there is a roof over your head and enough food to eat. But what happens when push comes to shove? Maybe none of us really knows how we would respond in "terrible" circumstances until they occur. Likely, most of us in the United States would have a hard time starving in the streets if we tried to though. We could literally go out and try to starve to death in the streets and probably end up in jail for loitering or starving in public. We'd get a nice cell to relax in and three square meals a day. I don't mean to be flippant or make this funny, but it sort of is. In reality, you can probably never *really* know how "enlightened" a person is until they are on the verge of death. Death is the ultimate "problem". How much can poverty and starvation bother you if you are absolutely unafraid to die?

The experience of nondual consciousness is the experience of total abundance. I have no idea how or if my particular consciousness will manifest as anything tangible or useful in "the world" anymore. The fact of the matter is I no longer really care about wealth beyond the absolute necessities. Forget about any "Secrets". I am not a "co-creator" and I could no longer even hold enough interest to try and manifest anything in particular, unless Mother Consciousness wants it so. I'm probably not even respectable enough to qualify as the CEO of a hot dog stand at this point, let alone a kick ass business dude. And yet, this is my reality: I am abundance itself in the hands of Mother Consciousness; ready to live or die as she might please. Forget about a retirement plan. Forget about what anybody else thinks. This kind of talk is no doubt scary shit for most people and it is a total paradigm shifting "fuck this game" for me.

"The experience of nondual consciousness is the experience of total abundance."

How can you suffer if there's nothing left that you want? How can you lack anything if you realize you are all that exists? Once we begin to examine the bars that comprise our cage, we will begin to notice something funny: our hands go right through the bars. The entire cage is a hologram made out of mind stuff. But in order to ever notice this you have to *really* want out. All of the millions of "co creators" out there are merely trying to manifest neat shiny things into their holographic cages. Show me an enlightened person that *really* wants something in particular and I'll show you a total charlatan. The wealthiest person in the world is playing with pebbles if he does not recognize the totality of the Kingdom of God: the absolute abundance that is Mother Consciousness.

Chapter Seven

Nebraska

GRANDPA

Hands that had raised ten kids;
they were a farmer's hands, fingers rough and thick.
The lacquer on the dining room table
was worn thin from where he slapped his hand playing cards.
He was the head of the family,
the hub of our little flock.
Now that he's gone, who could step up to take his place?
There in Nebraska, in the summer night sky,
the stars shone bright and clear.
The veil between this and that
grew thinner every moment that I watched.
I learned more from this catholic farmer
than from anyone I have ever known.
His devotion was breathtaking,
he called Mother Consciousness "God".

N ebraska was an awesome place for a city kid to visit. My grandfather had a farm of about 600 acres which was immense to a little boy. It was invigorating just to stand there in the lawn and see the sky stretched out in every direction as far as the eye could see. There were no ten story buildings, no traffic or urban sprawl. All I could see was nature all around me; nature and these funny people called relatives.

There on the farm I got to do things that I had never done in the city. At five years old I learned how to spit on the front porch of my grandpa's house. Lessons were provided free of charge by one of my comedian uncles. My mom was livid for days afterward, as apparently my uncle had neglected to teach me how or when I should stop spitting. I learned how to shoot a .22 rifle, a pistol and a shotgun at around age eleven. On another summer visit, at age thirteen, I took my first sip of whisky. Grandpa Hoffman must have doubled over with laughter watching the city kid's face turn green. On that same visit, I woke up one morning to find that one of my aunts, who I had had a disagreement with over something or another the previous day, had taken all of my underwear and hung them in the branches of the old oak tree at the side of the house. Those were fun times. I learned quickly you had to keep an eye on those aunts and uncles.

I learned how to play pinochle, the official family card game that summer. I spent hours and hours playing cards, sometimes just with grandpa, sometimes with aunts, uncles, cousins and family friends. It was an amazing feeling being surrounded by so much family. As an only child who had grown up in the city, being with extended family in Nebraska was nourishing to the soul. It seemed funny that it should have been so odd to be surrounded by a group of open hearted caring individuals. Looking back to those happy days I can see the appeal of satsang[5] for modern day spiritual seekers and I understand why people

---

[5] *Satsang* (Sanskrit sat=true, sanga=company) (1) the company of the

flock by the thousands to join spiritual groups. I understand why religion has been a bastion of civilization from the earliest beginnings of human culture. Everyone is looking for acceptance, safety, love and a comfortable oasis in a hostile world.

Here in the cities we seem to have more artificial barriers between us than they do in the countryside. We seem to have lost our connection to one another more starkly and completely, and the extended families that used to be the norm are becoming a rarity in our modern culture. As my generation's grandparents pass away, the move toward nuclear families and the death of the extended family seems to be our general direction. The haven that I used to have in the Nebraska countryside is there no longer; at least not in the way it was when Grandpa Hoffman was around.

"The illusion of separation is fueled by fear and the constant tension of never quite feeling comfortable and safe."

The more crowded it gets here in the cities the greater the illusion of separation seems to get. The illusion of separation is fueled by fear and the constant tension of never quite feeling comfortable and safe. Sitting around my grandfather's big oak dining room table with the aunts, uncles and cousins was like a nourishing sanctuary. It was satsang with whiskey and a pinochle deck and Grandpa Hoffman was our beloved guru.

Grandpa Hoffman was an impressive man, even back then, when he was in his seventies. He had come to America from Germany in the 1920's with his parents when he was around six years old. They settled in Nebraska and took up the family tradition of farming. Grandpa Hoffman made it all the way through middle school before quitting to work full time on the family farm. He had learned everything he needed to know school-wise to get through life by the age of fourteen and that was that. Grandpa Hoffman was fairly worldly wise for a

---

"highest truth," (2) the company of a *guru*, or (3) company with an assembly of persons who listen to, talk about, and assimilate the truth.

farmer from Nebraska, due no doubt in part to the fact that he had raised ten children with his wife, Grandma Hoffman. He had an obvious intelligence, a warm sense of humor and the uncanny ability to look you in the eye and know straight away when you were lying.

When I was 15 years old and going to high school in Southern California, I started getting into trouble. I started drinking and smoking pot and began getting into fist fights at school. My mother not knowing what to do with me, decided to send me back to Nebraska for awhile to live with the only person she knew could handle my punk ass: Grandpa Hoffman. I was secretly relieved at the prospect. I had never felt so safe and welcome in a place as I had in Nebraska on Grandpa Hoffman's farm. Even then, somewhere in my heart I knew that in reality life wasn't meant to be harsh and cruel. The mania and strangeness of growing up as an only child in the city had been getting the better of me. I didn't seem to fit in anywhere and the isolation felt alien and wrong.

And so I shipped off for the farm. I enrolled in the local high school, in a town with a population of about 300. It was interesting times. It was slower there but the people were somehow more down to earth and real. I noticed that I ate more when I was in Nebraska. Life there was more about real things; substantial things, and people took the time to sit and eat meals together as an essential part of daily life. I thought I was pretty big stuff back when I first shipped off to live in Nebraska; all city-like and sophisticated and whatnot, but I was really just a scared kid who welcomed and treasured the support of a loving extended family and the nourishing feeling of safety of Grandpa Hoffman's farm.

Evenings were spent with mostly just me and Grandpa Hoffman. We'd eat dinners comprised mostly of meat, potatoes, corn, bread, baked beans and the occasional "rabbit food". That was what he called lettuce and most other vegetables. Left over scraps were brought out to the front porch and dumped into a big steel pan as he yelled, "Here kitty, kitty, kitty!" The barn cats would come running three and four at a time to partake in the feast. After dinner we usually played pinochle while he would regale me with tales of his life as a farmer, his boyhood antics and old friends and relatives past and present. He had loads of outlandish and funny stories to tell about life on the farm and the shenanigans that my aunts and uncles had gotten into growing up. Once in awhile if he had had a shot of brandy or two, he'd even bring out the accordion and sing some old German folk songs. Other times we would just sit in recliners watching sitcoms or game shows. My Grandma Hoffman had died when I was five, about ten years earlier so it was just me and Grandpa. We were a couple of bachelors living off the fat of the land. We got along like gangbusters and had a riot of a time.

When I was old enough to get my driving permit, Grandpa Hoffman began teaching me how to drive in his old ford pickup, out in the pastures and on the gravel roads. He never hesitated to point out how rapidly I was approaching a turn or how I should be holding the steering wheel with both hands placed exactly at ten and two o'clock. Every Sunday morning we'd be up by 6:00 a.m. and ready to head to church by 7:15 a.m. No matter how late I had stayed up with friends the night before, I knew that when I smelled bacon and coffee I had better get up quick. Grandpa was never late to church and it was curtains for anyone running behind schedule. He had a pretty strong opinion when it came to Catholicism. When he found out I had never gone to catechism and earned my first communion, I was sent to Sunday school at the tender age of 15.

Catechism classes were held at the house of Father Smulowitz who lived in town right next to the church. During our lessons I asked Father Smulowitz plenty of intelligent and unanswerable questions regarding theology. Many times I was simply told it was a mystery and that God worked in mysterious ways. I would scrunch up my face, sigh and try to let it go.

"Father, how is it that God would create a world full of war, hatred and dishonesty?" I asked.

"God created man in his image," replied Father Smulowitz, "but he gave man freewill to serve him or to sin against him as he sees fit. The sinners pave their own way to hell, and the righteous will join the Father in the Kingdom of Heaven." Father Smulowitz spoke in a quiet voice with a thick Lithuanian accent. He was one of the kindest and gentlest men I had ever known.

I was excited when I had finally completed my studies many months later. I was scheduled to receive my first communion along with several other boys, all significantly younger than me. I remember being self conscious about not having a suit to wear to the first communion ceremony. As I slumped in one of the chairs by the big oak dining room table, sadly eyeing my casual city clothes, Grandpa Hoffman looked at me and said, "Michael, man makes the clothes. Clothes have never made the man."

I looked at him and nodded and that was that. We climbed into his Buick and headed down the gravel road toward church. As usual on drives through the country, Grandpa Hoffman pointed out the sections of land he had helped farm, parcels he had owned, sold and the one's he should've bought, and he named off the families who where currently working each section of land. The first communion ceremony and mass came and went and I was officially much more of a Catholic than I had been before. I was now authorized to join in communion: the sharing of the holy sacrament: a wafer and a sip of wine symbolizing the body and blood of Jesus Christ.

I look back fondly on the precious time spent with Grandpa Hoffman on his farm. He was a straight forward, no nonsense kind of guy and he taught me much of what it meant to be a man in this world. Grandpa Hoffman got to know all of my foibles rather quickly. He knew I used to sneak out to the old grain shed to smoke cigarettes in the mornings and sometimes in the evenings.

"Dammit Michael," he said, "If you're going to smoke, I just assume you do it on the front porch instead of sneaking around the shed. You're liable to blow yourself up flicking cigarette butts next to that old diesel truck."

That happy sophomore year came and went and I went back to California to finish my Junior and Senior year. I quickly fell back in with the same kind of alternative stoner crowd that I had befriended at my first high school. Thanks to my Nebraska experience however, I was a much more down to earth and grounded stoner punk than I used to be; imbued with a composed sort of Midwestern Zen. I was back trying to find a niche in the zoo of big-city high school culture, and somehow the stoner crowd still seemed to be the only place where I fit in and wasn't judged. They were all misfits like me: highly intelligent kids that didn't buy into the artificially segmented cliques and didn't give a shit about popularity. They were my new rag-tag satsang, but it was less nourishing and we were without a wise leader. We were just a bunch of knuckleheads commiserating over the insanity of the world, smoking bong loads and finding solace in the shared realization that society was a joke.

Grandpa Hoffman died about 20 years later, as I write this, just last year; at the tender age of 96. At his memorial, one by one, relatives who wanted to were allowed to stand up and tell fond stories of times they had spent with Grandpa Hoffman. I didn't think I could do it. I was too torn up and weeping pretty heavily. But somehow, without really deciding to, I stood up during a break in the action and walked to the front of the pews. Grandpa Hoffman had meant too much to me for me to let him go without a fitting tribute story. I recounted a time when I was 13 years old, creeping through the snow on Grandpa's farm with a .22 rifle, like Elmer Fudd from the old Bug's Bunny cartoons. I spotted a rabbit about 200 yards away, took aim and shot. I never thought I had a chance of hitting it from that far away. To my surprise I saw the rabbit fly into the air a few feet and then land dead. I ran over, picked it up by the ears and excitedly took it back to the farm house. It turned out to be a jack rabbit. I was torn between feeling proud of myself and feeling fiendish and sinister as it was the first creature I had ever shot and it was rather cute and fuzzy. I walked into the covered porch and yelled excitedly for Grandpa Hoffman to come see what I had got. When Grandpa Hoffman made it to the porch, he looked at the rabbit and then at me.

"Alright," he said, "now you're going to skin it, gut it and we're going to cook it for dinner."

That experience was pretty gruesome to a 13 year old city kid with no experience in such things. All of my food had always come from boxes and out of the freezers from the supermarket. The epitome of my culinary skill as a kid was being able to microwave something without blowing it to smithereens. I'm sure I must have gagged several times before I was through skinning and gutting that rabbit in the basement. When we had finally finished preparing and frying the rabbit up it tasted absolutely awful. It must have been a very old jack rabbit and he had probably been limping off to die somewhere in the trees before I put him out of his misery. The meat was tough and chewy with a flavor like burnt hair. That was the last thing I ever shot. It had been enough for me. Grandpa Hoffman taught me to never waste a thing and once again, I had learned my lesson.

I finished telling my story amidst streaming tears and sobs and went back to take my chair. His passing had hit me really hard. It was the first in a series of traumatic events that took place that year: the year that I fell into my pit of despair, ego dissolution crusade.

It seemed that Grandpa Hoffman was one of the last lynch pins holding my personal identity in place. In him I had found a rock of a man to whom I had tethered myself emotionally. He was the hub of an extended family that seemed to be the only place I had ever really belonged. Without him the bets were off. Our family, like most, would probably drift into the isolation of a bunch of nuclear families without a lot in common and without a central hub. As an adolescent and a teenager, the only place I had ever come really close to fitting into this world was there on Grandpa Hoffman's farm.

It is undoubtedly our deepest longing to feel permanently loved, at peace and safe. The reality is that lasting peace and contentment is ultimately something that must be discovered within our own individual consciousness through one-pointed introspection. Grandpa Hoffman was an example of a man who had found a deep connection to God and was able to extend his warmth and self assurance to those around him tangibly. In his later years he had no agenda, no ambitions and was content to live a simple life in the old farm house he had grown up on. When he reached his 90's though, as senile dementia began to set in, even Grandpa Hoffman began at times to get confused, irritated and afraid. There were still layers of mind stuff that had not been worked through. This is why it is crucial for each of us to go beyond our personalities; beyond our memories, thoughts and emotions altogether. It is not until we have stripped our egos down to the very barest minimum and become intimate with consciousness itself that we will find unfailing and irrevocable consolation.

"It is not until we have stripped our egos down to the very barest minimum and become intimate with consciousness itself that we will find unfailing and irrevocable consolation."

We must do this for ourselves. No one can hand it to us. To the degree that we have found our own connection with Mother Consciousness and assuming it is our lot, we in turn can mirror her absolute warmth and assurance as a beacon for those around us. In the eyes of God there is no real separation and all beings are welcome to the extent they can drop their defenses and go inward with perseverance. Those of us who succeed in reconnecting with Mother Consciousness completely will be the ones most qualified to share this safety and warmth with others. My grandfather, a farmer from Nebraska, succeeded to a large degree within the paradigm of Catholicism. It is the ultimate endeavor for any individual to take it all the way; to peel back the limits of duality, by any means necessary; fervently, until they no longer exist.

Chapter Eight

The Full Monty

THE GARDEN OF THE REAL

All day long I tend to this garden:
the garden of the real,
sprung forth from the dung pile
of this hollow worldly life.
Good manure is never wasted
on those who would grow into truth.
We smell the futility and begin to fall back,
like supernovas crashing in upon ourselves.
All day long now it's silence falling inward.
My heart full of peace,
I just nod like a fool.
I listen to silence,
the language of light:
flash, flash,
have no doubt,
we are only One.
These bodies are only fertilizer
in the garden of the real.

At the end of summer one of my best friends from California came to visit. Monty and I had been in college together some sixteen or seventeen years ago and had remained good friends since that time. I picked him up from the airport and brought him back to the house. After showing him around, we went up to the back deck to take in the view and catch up on life.

"So how's the family?" I asked.

"Yeah everything's good," Monty replied. "The kids are mostly staying with my mom during the week so me and Lacey can work."

"Oh? How's that going?"

"Yeah it's O.K. except my mom's starting to rub off on Hubert."

"I still can't believe you named your own kid Hubert."

"That was his grandfather's name. Besides he's o.k. with it, his friends call him Bert."

"Well what do you mean your mom's starting to rub off on him?" I asked.

"Now he's starting to see dead people."

"Oh, so your mom thinks she sees dead people?"

"Yeah, she talks to them too," replied Monty.

"You might start seeing dead people too then," I said. "It's probably genetic."

"Yeah right,"

"Yeah, you'll probably be in the bathroom trying to masturbate and a ghost will show up to haunt you," I laughed.

"Haunt this mutha fucka!" Monty howled making obscene back and forth hand gestures.

"Forget about the Ghost Busters, Monty's on the case!" I hooted and we both broke into uproarious laughter.

"So how are you guys liking it here?" asked Monty after the giggles had died down.

"It's pretty good," I replied.

"I was bummed when you moved," he said.

"Yeah it was hard to leave everybody behind."

"I miss our talks. There's no one I can really talk to about things with anymore."

"I miss hanging out too. How are you and Lacey doing?" I asked.

Monty was one of the first in our group of friends to get married. He and Lacey had been dating pretty exclusively since she was in high school and got married shortly after she had finished college. Neither one of them ever had time to really mature and find themselves or even date other people before getting hitched, and now thirteen years later, it was still a recurring theme: Monty was wondering if maybe he had somehow missed out on something.

"We're doing O.K. But I feel like our friendship isn't as strong as it could be. It seems like it's all kind of day to day routine," Monty said.

"Well what kinds of stuff do you guys talk about?" I asked.

"Mostly finances and kids, where we're gonna go on vacation... family stuff."

"Oh."

"Yeah, never anything deep or real...I can't help but wonder sometimes, I mean if we didn't have the kids, if we wouldn't both be happier with other people."

"If you're not happy now do you really think you're going to find happiness with another person?" I asked.

"Well yeah... I mean I could, you know, with someone more compatible; someone who shared the same interests and stuff. I guess Lacey's trying at least. She'll go to the brew pub and have a beer with me but I know she'd rather be at some swanky restaurant with exotic foods, drinking expensive wine," Monty replied.

"That's more than a lot of people get. It sounds like she's trying to compromise."

"Yeah, but I just can't help but wonder if I might not be happier with..."

"I think you're copping out," I interrupted. "Lacey's trying and you're fantasizing. If you're looking for real happiness, that's a solo adventure anyhow. The more you work on your own truth and happiness, the more you'll set an example for Lacey and the happier you'll both be."

"You need to water your grass man," Monty replied. "You've got some big, dry, brown patches over there," he said pointing.

Monty had a habit of changing topics very abruptly anytime he got uncomfortable in a conversation. He also sometimes did it to test people out and to see if he could get a rise out of them. The redirection worked on most people, people with short attention spans, but it had never worked on me. Most people went ahead and changed topics when redirected or else like me, they would just get irritated. I noticed though that where that particular trait had always pissed me off in the past, now I had no reaction.

"Watch your thoughts, the one's that tell you that you should be somewhere else doing something else or in a different situation."

"Yeah, that's just like you," I replied.

"What do you mean?"

"You're sitting here on this deck with a gorgeous view all around you and you're focused on the brown patches in the grass."

"Well it's not that simple," Monty protested.

"Actually it is. Take your focus off of Lacey, look at yourself closely and see if the cause of your unhappiness isn't in your own mind. Watch your thoughts, the one's that tell you that you should be somewhere else doing something else or in a different situation."

"Yeah but it's not just about the brown grass or the green grass, sometimes I wonder if I want a lawn at all. Maybe I want some fruit trees or,"

"Still copping out," I interrupted again. "Forget about lawns and fruit trees. You won't be happy until you find out what it is that is telling you that your happiness lies somewhere else with someone else.

You've got to trace back those thoughts and pin down whatever it is that lies behind them."

"Yeah I see what you're saying," Monty admitted. "See that's what I miss. Our conversations make me think."

⚜

Personal relationships are one of the primary arenas where many people mistakenly believe true happiness can be found. Our culture especially hypes romantic relationships as a panacea for all of an individual's ills. Modern pop music and romantic movies unabashedly push the idea that finding one's perfect match and soul mate is the end all, be all of true happiness. If you could only find "the one" they say, you would live happily ever after. But it just ain't so.

When you're in a relationship, even a great relationship, the mind has a tendency to wonder if there isn't something or someone better for you out there, or if you wouldn't be happier being single. When you're single the mind longs to find that special someone to fill the void. It's the same old no win situation that Maya loves to perpetuate as a possible solution to lasting happiness in the illusory dualistic world. It's the same tired carrot on a stick game, but it's one that has been emphasized and cherished since the beginning of modern culture. Perhaps the roles are changing. Maybe there isn't as much pressure in today's society to settle down and get married as there was in the past. But the idea of finding happiness in a romantic relationship is still as revered as it's ever been.

To believe that you can find happiness in a relationship if you haven't yet found happiness for yourself is just another form of denial though. Find lasting happiness for yourself and you will automatically begin drawing other happy type people into your world. Realize nondual consciousness for yourself, and you will begin drawing other nondual type people into your world. If you can abide in nondual consciousness, whether you have a romantic relationship or not, you will always be at peace.

Many of today's spiritual seekers are now looking to spiritual gurus to fill the void that other relationships have failed to satiate. This is just an even more pronounced form of denial in which you are still giving your personal power away to an outside authority, hoping that they will be able to magically bestow contentment upon you. The spiritual marketplace of today is rife with gurus and "enlightened masters" who promise to heal your emotional wounds and ensure your salvation for a price. The market place is so lucrative because the majority of us have grown up in less than supportive environments, and many of us are still looking for the perfect mommy or daddy figure to make everything all right. Someone who claims to be "God realized" can become the ultimate authority figure for a spiritual seeker. I've seen and heard of plenty of people being taken advantage of by would be gurus who use their spiritual clout to fulfill their worldly desires. The emotional fallout that comes with recognizing your guru is just a pervert or a shyster can be devastating. Ultimately you must always rely on Mother Consciousness directly. The charlatan guru gig is one of Maya's nastiest and most heinous playgrounds. There are thousands, probably hundreds of thousands of people who are not enlightened but who dress up in fancy costumes, have spiritual names and claim themselves as spiritual authorities based on such and such lineage. Here's the shtick in a nutshell:

1. I've attained something magical and mystical which you do not have and which you cannot attain without my intercession.
2. I'm something holier than you; an emissary of God, who has been sent to this muddy earth pond to care for all you poor spiritual guppies with my omnipotent grace and benevolence.
3. I have a set of spiritual tenets that you must adhere to in order to be granted salvation. I more than likely also have some mystical exercises that will purify your body and mind, and

prepare you for the ultimate enlightenment. I will bestow this enlightenment upon you later, on the behalf of God, based on your worthiness and when you are ready.

4. I will grant you all of this and more for the low, low price of X amount of dollars. I take cash and most major credit cards, no personal checks please.

5. In lieu of sufficient money or personal possessions, I may still be persuaded to intervene on your behalf if you donate your life energy to working for my organization and spreading my cause. And/or if I find you sufficiently attractive, I may allow you to have divine, holy sex with me, which will also purify your body and soul and prepare you for the eventual bestowal of enlightenment.

Look at these games closely. Don't ever give the power of your happiness away to another individual regardless of their promises or spiritual status. It is a losing proposition. Lasting happiness, peace and abidance in nondual consciousness are your birthright and the innermost core of what you already are. You have but to search inside your own consciousness with a sufficient amount of dedication to reach this truth. It has always been inside of you and no outside authority will ever be needed to find it. There are some people that have the capability to point the way accurately but they generally don't ask for anything in return. The ones that are pointing the way authentically aren't running any games; they have nothing to gain or lose. They don't run out seeking students and they have no opinion as to whether you stay and listen or go away.

"Lasting happiness, peace and abidance in nondual consciousness are your birthright and the innermost core of what you already are."

The authentic spiritual teacher knows that your truth is as valid as that of any enlightened master past or present. It is here for you now, wherever you are, and not necessarily in India, China, Tibet or the

Himalayas. Someone abiding in nondual consciousness exudes truth from their very pores. It is not something that they turn on and off and it's not something they can actively deny or bestow on anyone else. All they can do is point for those that are willing to look, and the direction they are pointing is always inward.

Don't get fooled by the lovey-dovey nirvana in twelve easy steps sales pitch. Awakening to truth is often a messy business that has only to do with cutting asunder emotional and mental crap. The spiritual game is one of Maya's favorite games of all. She encourages people to adorn their ego masks with beautiful spiritual markings. In fact she'd love for you to run out and change your name to something spiritual; something Indian, Chinese or Japanese. That would make her smile. And if you adopted some really pretty spiritual garb to go with your new name and spiritual affiliation, Maya would clap and giggle like a little child on Christmas morning.

To abide in nondual consciousness is to be less than naked. It has nothing to do with adding anything on. It is being nameless and in a state of no separation. You don't become someone special. On the contrary, you become no one at all. The real spiritual master is someone who has faded into practically nothing; not necessarily the one with the winning smile and impeccable clothing.

There is no room in nondual consciousness for better or worse spiritual paths or religions, just as there is no room in nondual consciousness for believing that any relationship whatsoever holds the key to your eternal happiness. There is only one relationship that is worth exploring in this regard: it is the relationship between your consciousness and itself.

When you endeavor to find Absolute Reality via nondual consciousness, you will yourself become a light that helps other people illuminate their own inner truth. From that space you will never be disappointed in relationship because there will be nothing that you really require from any other person. Finding Absolute Reality; finding

God for ourselves, is actually the greatest gift we could ever give to those around us. It is from the vantage point of nondual consciousness that we can reflect to others the greatest potential that each of us has: the ability to find everlasting contentment for ourselves.

CHAPTER NINE

A Bad Case of Spiritualitis

PUPPET LIFE

Time carries us like a river made of God.
God shines through us;
we are totally immersed.
In the funny play of life
there are no rehearsals.
The good news is you cannot get it wrong.
Light shines through us
and we do a puppet dance.
We are divinity in motion
returning to our source.
We are only energy expanding and contracting:
puppets seeking freedom
that was never really lost.

I really began to get serious about my spiritual journey after the acid experience in my early twenties. I stopped hanging out with my stoner high school friends and adopted a health regimen based on ancient Taoist practices. I began getting up at four in the morning to practice Tai Chi and to meditate before my day began. My breakfasts, like most of my meals, consisted mostly of mung beans, tofu, rice, greens and other assorted vegetables. I scoffed at people who were eating "the standard American diet," S.A.D. I quit drinking and smoking all together and began taking a variety of herbal and vitamin supplements. I practiced celibacy as an ideal, believing that I could transmute my sexual essence into an indestructible spiritual body and thereby attain spiritual immortality. At a certain point, after much spiritual cultivation, I was supposed to be able to create a spiritual embryo that would pop out from the top of my head, marking me as an immortal being no longer confined to mundane worldly existence; free from the 'red dust of the world' as the Taoists called it. Aside from my academic studies, I read only spiritual texts and watched very little T.V.

I became so holy during that time that I even began lecturing other family members and friends on proper diet and the importance of physical, mental and spiritual hygiene. I was walking on a cloud and was undoubtedly superior to the majority of people who were mired in the dust of the world, lost in their inferior, mundane, habitual ways. When I'd go to the coffee shop with my friend Catherine to study and socialize, I'd tell her about the evils of gulping down coffee as I gracefully sipped my green tea in a most delicate fashion, savoring the aroma and taste with far too much self satisfaction. When I looked into the mirror in those days, I was sure that there must be a halo beginning to form around my head. Every once and awhile I'd feel the tiniest itch on my upper back where I imagined I would shortly be sprouting angelic wings. I guarantee I was a world class spiritual asshole; completely full of shit.

How many people have you met like that? People who are so

enmeshed in their extraneous spiritual practices that they believe their enlightenment is predicated by them. It is a common malady, frightening to behold and extremely difficult to get rid of. I like to call it spiritualitis. Spiritualitis translates as inflammation of the spirit. The idea of spirit, like everything else that exists in the world of duality; is just that: an idea. Like the rest of the universe, it is an emanation of your mind. Inflammation of the spirit happens when you place too much importance on the concept. There are many schools of "spiritual mysticism" that would have you running around and practicing various exercises in order to perfect yourself, and to ready you for some spiritual achievement that is supposed to take place somewhere down the road, at some other time and after you've done X amount of *japas*, mantras or jumping jacks. The problem is that the carrot on the stick that Maya is dangling in front of you, actually leans further away when you're standing on your head or twisted into a "bird of paradise" yoga pose.

Spiritualitis is one of the most treacherous and deadly of Maya's many maladies. By comparison, people who are mired in religion or philosophy (which we'll touch on later) are not nearly as grotesque. Spiritualitis is deadly because it can be quite elusive and difficult to diagnose. People suffering from its ill effects cannot always be easily seen coming from a mile away, unlike people who are deeply entrenched in religion and philosophy. Spiritualitis can be extremely evasive and elusive. You might even be good friends with someone who is suffering from it and never even notice that they are looking down on you from a pedestal positioned well outside the stratosphere. Not all people suffering from spiritualitis put on fancy robes or costumes or change their name to "Ananda," "Turiya" or "Mokshashanti". Oh no, I'm afraid it can be much more deceptive than that. Spiritualitis is one of the most refined and therefore most binding of Maya's traps. It is the

"Inflammation of the spirit happens when you place too much importance on the concept."

fortifying of the ego mask with elitist spiritual beliefs, practices and affiliations.

When I first met Christina, she was flirting with membership in a Krishna based group in Los Angeles. After we had been dating for awhile I agreed to go check out the group with her. We entered the spiritual teacher's house, where most of the group meetings took place and Christina took me around to meet various acquaintances of hers within the group. Most of the people seemed genuinely good natured. I could see the appeal of membership right away. Here was a warm, seemingly open group of people who would accept you wholeheartedly if you would only agree to adhere to their beliefs. Some of them had various spiritual names and were dressed in quasi Hindu garb.

The meeting began with chanting and later moved on to ecstatic dancing with Indian music and singing. I was actually having a good time. The devotional nature of the singing and chanting was lovely. As the music and singing reached a frenzied climax, people were twirling around and hopping up and down with their hands in the air and I was nearly compelled to bust out some of my old break dance maneuvers from grade school. But Christina and my relationship was too new to risk it and so I fought back the urge with some effort.

After the meeting, while most of the guests were venturing outside to partake in a vegetarian potluck, Christina introduced me to the eldest son of the main spiritual teacher. He and I fell into a bit of spiritual discussion and I probed him into spelling out some of the finer points of their teachings for me. While I hadn't at that time gone through any final ego unmasking, I was well enough versed in the conceptual and philosophical aspects of most of the main spiritual teachings to hold my own in a spiritual discussion with nearly anyone.

While questioning him about the nature of ultimate reality, I was not at all surprised to find out that because they worshiped Krishna, God was thought to be a blue light, with which the spiritual aspirant was to eventually merge at the culmination of their spiritual journey. This was of course, only to be attained after a lifetime's worth of chanting, reciting mantras and devotion to the teachers and to Krishna. There didn't seem to be any clear notion of Krishna being your innermost nature. Krishna was a deity, apart from you, and it was through utmost devotion to him that upon your death, you would be transported to his realm to abide with him forever. It sounded like another version of the same old heaven story to me. There didn't seem to be any notion of methodically stripping one's self down to nothing, but only of transforming one's self into something else and then launching this something toward the holy blue light at the end.

In all fairness, I do recognize a genuine *bhakti*[6] tradition as a valid means of achieving abidance in nondual consciousness. And I would say that many of the world's religions could be considered *bhakti* traditions. One-pointed devotion toward a deity is much better than being energetically scattered as far as spiritual progress goes. But I think there is a critical fine line between thinking there is a power outside yourself that is going to help you and recognizing that divinity is the ultimate core of what you already are. I speculate that it is a fine line that many a *bhakta* has faltered on.

In those days, Christina was teaching yoga at the local college, having earned a teaching certificate through one of the teachers at the Krishna group. During one her first classes, Christina explained the meaning of yoga as "the union of mind and body." She didn't mention spirit because she wanted to leave the esoteric aspects out of it. It was a college course filled with pretty co-eds whose main concern was a

---

[6]*Bhakti, devotion* or *portion*[1] in practice signifies an active involvement by the devotee in divine worship. The term is often translated as "devotion," though increasingly "participation" is being used as a more accurate rendering, since it conveys a fully engaged relationship with God.[2] One who practices *bhakti* is called a *bhakta*,[3] while *bhakti* as a spiritual path is referred to as *bhakti marga*, or the *bhakti* way.[4][5] *Bhakti* is an important component of many branches of Hinduism, defined differently by various sects and schools.[6]

tighter butt and better abs rather than spiritual development. Another of the Krishna devotees that was enrolled in Christina's class at the college confronted Christina after the class. She was horrified at the omission of spirit from Christina's definition of yoga.

"What if the souls of these girls aren't saved and they never devote themselves to Krishna because of your inadequate teaching?" she asked accusingly.

In another class, Christina mentioned to her students that yoga could also be used as a moving meditation, much like Tai Chi. Again the Krishna devotee that was in her class was horrified. Apparently Tai Chi was not a sanctioned means of union with Krishna and therefore should not have been compared with yoga in any way. Rather than confront Christina directly this time, the Krishna devotee spoke to one of the main teachers of the Krishna group who later called Christina on the phone. The spiritual teacher essentially told her that if she continued to mislead the yoga class so egregiously, she would undoubtedly be subject to much bad karma and all chance of union with Krishna would be void. That's when Christina told them, "thank you very much, and goodbye."

"Anyone with the proper motivation and tenacity can reach the depths of ultimate truth with some very basic tools."

Spiritualitis is the insidious malady that plagues all of the fake gurus and spiritual masters that are lurking out there in the spiritual market place. By extension, it is contracted by their followers as well. If you detect any elitism whatsoever in someone's teachings it should start to set off your bullshit detector immediately. I'm not saying that correct spiritual practice is effortless, but I am saying that is most definitely not exclusive. Anyone with the proper motivation and tenacity can reach the depths of ultimate truth with some very basic tools.

Spiritualitis feeds off of elitism. In nearly any chat room that is focused on spiritual topics you will find people spouting off their theoretical knowledge and touting their lineage of teachers as the ultimate authority. You can smell the stench of spiritualitis in most of the spiritual books and audio c.d.'s on the market today. The smell of spiritualitis can be difficult to detect to the untrained nose however. Most teachers cover it up with profuse doses of compassion talk perfume. They'll usually say their teaching is the best, not blatantly, but insinuating it strongly. Then they'll tell you it is their job to bring these teachings to humanity by virtue of their overabundant compassion and humility. If you follow their lead and cast them in a radiant, holier than thou light, so much the better.

Less virulent strains of spiritualitis can even be witnessed in your local yoga studio or meditation class. You'll see some people competing to hold their pose just a little more perfectly or keep their spine straighter than their neighbor. They'll be the one's wearing the most fashionable leotards or meditation garb and the ones that always have one eye on the teacher, waiting for some verbal acknowledgement or a pat on the head.

Other forms of spiritualitis can be harder to detect. Let's say "Mokshashanti" has paid $1,000 dollars for a high powered mantra from a super spiritual guru, that he recites silently and constantly to himself. Nobody would ever know about his secret spiritual practice or the incredible amounts of spiritual merit he was accruing, unless of course he told people about it. All you would see is "Mokshashanti's" ultra benevolent smirk as he gazed at you from his pedestal located just outside the stratosphere. He could just be standing in line at the grocery store or at the bank and you'd never know how spiritual he was; how far removed from the sad mass of people that didn't have a super potent mantra to recite. You would never even have an inkling that he was unique in any way, unless of course he was wearing a fancy costume or you knew his name was "Mokshashanti". That might be enough to tip you off to the fact that he was an elevated being.

You get the idea. The new age magazines are filled with the cheesy pictures of "enlightened" spiritual beings who are just bursting out of the page ready to balance you, *kundalini* you, *diksha* you and whatnot. If you ever get the bright idea to go to a new age festival you'd better bring some Pepto Bismol or a similar antacid. It's like braving some kind of creepy carnival freak show. In every other booth someone is channeling the ascended master Kadanumu or prophesying, either about of the coming golden age of humanity or the end of the world. You can literally feel the spiritual egos just oozing out of the booths toward you, beckoning you to come partake in their particular brand of holy crap.

The variations of spiritualitis are endless, and as of yet, no cure has been proven 100 percent effective. I used to suffer from it so I know how insidious it can be and how difficult it can be to overcome its debilitating effects. If you or a loved one suffers from spiritualitis don't worry, there is always hope. Try contacting a spiritualitis specialist immediately. In the meanwhile, as a stop gap measure, try administering a swift and hard kick to the buttocks; to be repeated as often as necessary until the patient regains their senses.

Chapter Ten

Time Honored Forms of Mental Constipation

INTO THE ABSTRACT

Life becomes open-ended
as you head into the abstract.
Time appears to move
but what you really are cannot change.
To release yourself into the abstract
you must let go of everything.
This is where real life begins
and we become unified, indistinguishable,
beyond our personalities.
There are no words that can describe
what you really are.
Words like limitless, boundless and eternal
are only fingers that untie mental knots.
When you release yourself
from bondage into the abstract,
you become a traveler stepping lightly,
illuminating shadows before they begin;
sun rising from the inside out; a child of perpetual dawn.

The search for truth is ultimately a personal journey inward. It is a journey of stripping down the layers of ego and mind until nothing remains except consciousness. Nondual consciousness is not to be found in personal relationships, gurus, the Far East or the Far West. Nondual consciousness is likewise not to be found in politics, the endeavor to create an enlightened society, metaphysics, philosophy, religion or any of Maya's other countless fascinating side shows.

If you want to talk to people on the "other side," you're wasting your time. Ghosts and spirits are best handled the way my friend Monty would handle them: drop trou and chase them away. When you abide in nondual consciousness, any separation between life and death becomes void. Everything, absolutely everything, is realized as consciousness and ghosts and spirits, like every other aspect of this world, are recognized as just an emanation of your mind. If you see ghosts or talk to dead people that's fine, but recognize it for what it is. It's just a figment of your imagination; another dream interaction, albeit with less substantial characters. Perhaps there are enlightened souls that get channeled and have some excellent things to say to humanity. They should be treated as would any enlightened teacher be treated, not with reverence and awe, but with an acknowledgement of your sameness and gratitude for the potential they mirror back to you. You are as holy as any exalted being who has ever existed or ever will exist.

Astrology is a side show that many people like to entertain themselves with. There are people out there who undoubtedly can tell you many things that will likely transpire in your future. But this is just the same as someone giving you the details of a dream before you have it. It might be interesting, but it won't necessarily help you transcend the dream state itself. Ultimately this is what we're looking to do: to transcend the dream of duality. And whether you're a Virgo, Gemini, born in the year of the rat or the monkey, the journey to nondual consciousness is the same. It involves transcending descriptions and limitations rather than focusing on or strengthening them.

Ceremonies, rituals, black and white magic are all in the same boat. No ideology can be spared if you're looking to experience Absolute Reality. Ceremonies and rituals can be useful for helping you to reconnect with your inner truth, but ultimate truth is best experienced continually as the only thing that exists. Using magic to create things or to alter and shape events is in the same category as the co-creation gig. It still requires belief in your personal dream character and the desire to make things other than the way they are. None of these things are wrong mind you; they're just not on point as far as abiding in nondual consciousness is concerned. Nondual consciousness is about experiencing the perfection of everything as it exists in this moment. It cannot be experienced while trying to manifest a jet plane, a pot of gold or the perfect mate. Abiding in nondual consciousness ultimately requires a total and complete surrender of all wants, needs, ideas and thoughts.

> "Everything is simply consciousness, and reality is always reality, regardless of what you think about it."

Philosophy is one of the bigger quagmires that many an intellectual jumps into head first. It is a mental description of truth that can only ever keep you separated from the experience of truth itself. We all know people that have memorized large volumes of philosophy or have particular stances, this way or that, that they can back up with endless amounts of philosophical quotations and text. What good could that possibly do when the experience of nondual consciousness lies completely beyond the intellect? Again, it reminds me of modern scientists and spiritual philosophers who busy themselves trying to come up with some all abiding "theory of everything." Why would you waste your time on such a thing? Everything is simply consciousness, and reality is always reality, regardless of what you think about it. Thinking about it only separates you from it. Absolute Reality is to be experienced as your fundamental truth and the truth of all that exists. And nondual consciousness cannot be experienced while the mind is spinning with theories, ideologies or thoughts period.

I am hard pressed to think of anything that would be less worthwhile than getting a graduate degree in philosophy. Hundreds of thousands of dollars and several years later, you'd emerge from your dorm room wearing a sweater tied over you shoulders and smoking a pipe; one eyebrow arched condescendingly. You'd be hungrily scanning the terrain for feeble prey that you could devour with the giant teeth of your dinosaur mind (by the way, if I'm ever in another music group the band name is now a toss up between Yolk of Consciousness and Dinosaur Mind). As you approached, people, even friends and relatives, would go running frantically in all directions. No one would even want to eat dinner with you anymore lest you go spouting off about Plato, Aristotle or Descartes. Small children would shriek and cry as you strode about with your one overambitious eyebrow permanently frozen in a questioning gaze, and you would be forever condemned to the realm of the intellectual undead; forced to wander the land with an insatiable appetite, feeding off of the inferiority of lesser intellects.

This brings us to one of the biggest sacred cows of all: Religion. Before I talk about religion let me first remind those who might be offended, that earlier I stated that I recognize a true *bhakti* tradition as a valid means of reaching nondual consciousness, and that many religions are by their nature, undoubtedly *bhakti* traditions. With that said, religion is noigiler spelled backwards. Noigiler doesn't really mean anything and in general, neither does religion; except to the extent that it is used as a jumping off point for a dedicated personal journey inward toward self realization.

What is religion except for a set of tenets, philosophies and stories imbued with strong emotions? Religions generally serve first and foremost, to divide the sinners from the saints and to make us feel as if we are part of an exclusive group of righteous and privileged people.

Follow our way or go to hell is a basic tenet of many religions. It's undoubtedly a good scare tactic that grips many a person in fear, but the enlightenment factor of such a tenet unfortunately scores around 0 on a scale from 1 to 10. As I mentioned previously, elitism is the hallmark of spiritualitis. Elitism is also a hallmark of most religions, just stated more blatantly and matter-of-factly.

If you look at the nature of religion realistically, it serves the same purpose as any other organization or institution: self preservation. It is a pieced together construct, held together by emotion that makes us feel as if we are somehow protected from the vastness of the universe simply by virtue of our membership. It is a construct that proposes to assuage our fears and answer the big questions of life, death, morality and truth, but on such a scale that it must be dumbed down to be palatable for the masses. The real agenda for such an institution—for most institutions—is control. Ironically, religions tend to foist their own brand of fear on their adherents in order to keep them loyal. Like any large side show in Maya's circus, the main objective of a religion is to perpetuate and preserve itself at all cost, and this is generally done by controlling its members with fear tactics.

Many religions rely on ancient fairy-tale like stories to give them cohesion and on which they base their authority. The upside of belonging to a religion, like most other organizations, is that it brings a sense of community and safety. As we've seen, sense of community and safety is a powerful driving force in the midst of the fragmented and neurotic societies that we find ourselves in today. Such community comes at a cost however. You have to believe in and uphold the tenets and fears of your religion. And those tenets and fears, like all other mental constructs, can serve to keep you separated from the simple, natural divinity and fundamental truth of your own existence. If you already experience nondual consciousness as your day to day reality, there is obviously no harm in participating in religion, but don't fool yourself. Truth is not exclusive. It has no viable creeds, mottos or tenets. Truth has absolutely nothing to do with fear and it can never be constrained by ideas or beliefs, no matter how sacred or ancient.

Religions can be useful as jumping off points when it comes time to undergo your authentic personal journey. Like all mental constructs they can point to a greater truth, but like all mental constructs they must be jettisoned entirely on your journey into Absolute Reality. It can be a bit of a bittersweet affair having to break through all of your mental constructs and cut through the philosophical and religious ideologies that have surrounded you all your life. But the bittersweet feeling will be rendered into only a faint nostalgia when you look back at your old mental constructs from the vantage point of nondual consciousness.

"It can be a bit of a bittersweet affair having to break through all of your mental constructs and cut through the philosophical and religious ideologies that have surrounded you all your life."

CHAPTER ELEVEN

The Return to Shangri-La

ANGELS IN THE MIDST

It's no secret
that truth is what I long for.
Here in the center of life,
I reconcile every tragedy and fear
of this world.
I trace every sound that I hear,
everything that I see, taste or feel
back to the source,
and revel in its absolute perfection.
We have only ever been
this stillness at the unchanging center:
perfection in the midst of death,
watching this parade.

According to a Jewish Hindu friend of mine we are about to enter the golden age of the *Mishegas Yuga*. Every man and woman will have abundant riches and perfect health. Violence will cease to exist on the planet altogether and universal brotherhood and sisterhood will emerge as the new paradigm from which we will cherish the holiness of each others beings more than we cherish ourselves. The very concepts of negativity, pain, hatred, discomfort and evil will vanish from human consciousness altogether. Every human being will live in perfect harmony and coexist in a rapturous dance of total ecstasy. And the mantra of *One Love* shall resound throughout the land for ever more until the end of time.

I'm just kidding. If you're one of those people that is waiting and praying for the coming golden age of humanity I'd say don't hold your breath. The world has been in relative chaos since the dawn of civilization and it's doubtful that it will be sorting itself out completely anytime soon. It's not really the point is it? At least it's not the point if your focus is on spiritual awakening and abiding in nondual consciousness.

Working toward world peace and a better place for the children is admirable but such things have little to do with real spiritual awakening. Real spiritual awakening—abiding in nondual consciousness—is about experiencing the background of reality and the perfection of the totality *as it is*. Perfection does not lie in a far off place sometime in the future but right here and right now, in the very depths of our own experience. The bottom line is that the experience of nondual consciousness cannot be had while your energy is tied into the world. It is a noble thing to want to change the world for the better, but for most, this is still just another of Maya's side shows that is used to avoid any deep internal work. I'm not saying that you shouldn't help to take care of people, animals and the planet in general as the opportunity naturally arises. These tendencies may actually occur more powerfully as you center yourself in the view of nondual consciousness. What I am saying is that it is egotistic to make a show out of your altruism. Martyring yourself for the world makes for a most impressive mask decoration. It makes for a very pretty mask that will be applauded by a great many people, granted you are changing the world in a direction that they approve of.

Look at most of the politicians out there. I imagine some of them actually start out enthusiastically with genuinely altruistic motives. But no matter how well-intentioned you are, engaging in politics is like walking into Maya's fortress. You might think you're going to light up the place with the torch of your righteousness, but your fire will begin to sputter out sooner or later, and Maya will start convincing you how much better it is in the darkness. She'll tell you that if you would only allow your vision to adjust to the darkness, you will become more powerful than you have ever imagined. Whether you are left wing or right wing, duality is the direction of the dark side.

"You can't just walk into Maya's fortress and start moving her stuff around without reproach."

Politics is by its very nature pedantic, ostentatious and lends itself to corruption. The people that get drawn into politics are often times, the least creative and least artistic people in our society. By and large they are people with a thirst for power and a penchant for controlling others rather than people with genuinely benevolent motives. Even if they don't start out corrupt and self serving, more than likely that is how they'll end up.

You can't just walk into Maya's fortress and start moving her stuff around without reproach. A truly benevolent politician with unbendable motives would have to maneuver around Maya's fortress with the utmost precision and caution to avoid getting shot or worse in this day and age. Honest Abe Lincoln, John F. Kennedy, Martin Luther King Jr., these all strike me as straightforward people who were probably trying to do the right thing for their country. Look what it got them. I say fight the power, but fight it from the inside out. The truth is that someone who is truly abiding in nondual consciousness generally wouldn't touch politics with a thousand foot pole. It is the nature of the dualistic world to be relatively out of control just as it is the nature of the human ego to be ever striving to control it.

Between six and seven thousand years ago many early humans began moving away from nomadic hunting and gathering lifestyles toward agriculture. Over time the fertile floodplains and valleys that lined the great Nile, Euphrates, Indus, Tiger and Yellow Rivers gave rise to the first city-states. As these new communities developed, systems of writing were created to help keep track of land, crops, livestock and business transactions. Social hierarchies were further developed and an elite group of rulers and priests began to spring up to preside over the newly created abundance of the now centralized and ever growing cities. Society became increasingly stratified into merchants, craftsmen, warriors, laborers and the ruling elite. As populations grew, the need for economic resources and more land led to the emergence of increased conflict and warfare with neighboring states. Now, thousands of years later, we seem to be the same old bunch of greedy power hungry bastards playing the same old petty war games. And as it has been since the dawn of civilization, a few percent of the world's elite still control most all of its resources.

It's funny that most people never step back from the world far enough to see what a repetitive joke it is. The idiot politicians that are all over the talk shows and television shows yelling at the camera and pushing their particular agendas are no different than the power mongers of thousands of years ago. The only difference is now they are wearing suits with red or blue neck ties instead of robes and crowns. Let's get real for a second. The name of the political game is power and money. It always has been and always will be about control: the ego's ultimate agenda.

The government is eternally placating us with one hand and handing us a bill with the other. I'm not saying that socialism isn't a viable paradigm for a healthy society, but to truly work it would require the cooperation of a group of benevolent and somewhat enlightened politicians. Here in the United States it seems that government continues to grow, even as the politicians give themselves raises and push special interest agendas that generally don't benefit the majority. There's a reason I mostly don't pay any attention to politics whatsoever: it will seriously mess with your head. Just for the fun of it though, I'm going to look up a couple of the top stories of the day to see what's going on around the nation and the world; to see if they might provide some further examples of the point I'm trying to make: politics and spiritual awakening are essentially mutually exclusive.

O.K. let's see here. On the front page of the newspaper we have, "State to get $274 million in U.S. aid". At the risk of playing the devil's advocate, where is the U.S. going to borrow their money from? As of right now the U.S. is already over 14 trillion dollars in debt, with Japan and China currently neck and neck as the largest owners of American debt at between 8 and 9 billion dollars each. Some economists go so far as to estimate that the amount of U.S. debt that China holds may actually be closer to 1.7 trillion dollars if you factor in debt purchased by partially state owned firms that is not readily transparent. I don't know about you but I think it might be high time to start learning some Mandarin.

Speaking of China, here's an unfortunate story: on page five we have, "School Rampage has Authorities Up in Arms." Apparently a 26 year-old man attacked a kindergarten in a suburb of Beijing, killing three children, a teacher and injuring seventeen others with a 24" knife. According to this article, this is the seventh such attack in China in the past four months, mostly involving middle aged men attacking young children in schools with, hammers, axes and knives.

Hmmm…what could be going on in the heads of these kinds of people? I don't mean to speculate blindly, but perhaps they could be feeling the pressure of being impoverished in a country where the unequal distribution of wealth is currently at a Gini coefficient[7] of roughly .5 and where human rights for the impoverished are less than sub par. Maybe they've lost their jobs or been evicted from their homes because the government and the ultra elite are amassing all the countries wealth voraciously, while leaving less fortunate citizens with almost no opportunity for right livelihood or even adequate food and shelter. Perhaps they are simply criminally insane and the government has no resources allocated to deal with them because they've filled their mental institutions with perfectly sane people who annoy them with petitions and grievances that interfere with their political agendas. I guess all I can say with certainty is that it doesn't sound like the kind of thing that happens when happy people are pleased with their lives and with their government.

The argument that spurred the Chinese citizens to adopt communism in the 1960's was largely that the overly educated bourgeois were unfairly controlling the nation's resources. Chairman Mao incited the poor and the disgruntled powerless youth and executed a ten year "cultural revolution" that effectively halted higher education in China. Citizens who were educated past middle school levels were largely targeted, stripped of possessions and sent away to the country side for "reeducation". Millions of people had their human rights annulled and as many as 3 million were killed during the "cultural revolution". Land owners were commonly labeled "revisionists" and persecuted; their lands confiscated by government.

It is an interesting note that during the "cultural revolution," Chairman Mao ordered much of China's wealth of historical, religious and spiritual artifacts destroyed. His argument was that such artifacts had their roots in the old ways of thinking and were therefore opposed to Marxist-Leninist and Maoist thinking. Religious persecution was rampant. As many as 6,000 temples were destroyed in Tibet alone.

---

[7]A measure of the income disparity between citizens in a given population.

Chairman Mao thought that his extreme form of government was incompatible with religion. How much more incompatible would it be with total spiritual awakening?

After over 40 years of a failed experiment in Communism, China's wealth distribution is now moving rapidly toward the exact opposite of the communist party's stated ideals. China is quickly developing into a country with one of the highest discrepancies of wealth and income between the ultra elite and the majority of its impoverished citizens, having recently surpassed the U.S. and topped only by South America, Mexico and parts of Africa[8].

> "As it has been from the dawn of civilization, the world is founded squarely on a belief in duality and the absolute division between us and them. We are not our brother's keepers."

As it has been from the dawn of civilization, the world is founded squarely on a belief in duality and the absolute division between us and them. We are not our brother's keepers. The stark mental and psychological division between human egos is what allows societies with such gross class distinctions. Taken to an extreme, the absolute conceptual division between egos is also what allows a disaffected citizen to break into a school and hack up little children in protest of a Nation's inequality. It is this false dichotomy of me/you, of us/them that allows for all the injustice and inhumanity that exist in this world. Without this false dichotomy it would be virtually impossible for someone to harm another person or even have bad feelings toward another. If all people were enlightened we actually would live in a Shangri-la where wealth distribution was more evenly apportioned, naturally and without the necessity of big government interference.

---

[8]I would like to point out that these statistics and numbers are rough and culled from several different sources. It is not my intention to render my arguments as extremely precise by academic standards, but only to make a general point within the context of our topic of spiritual awakening vs. the nature of the dualistic world.

Let's be honest about it. No government truly holds the people's welfare as its *primary* concern. Rather, like any large and powerful construct in Maya's domain, it seeks to preserve itself at all cost. The politicians themselves are cogs in a wheel; their main purpose? It is first and foremost to uphold the construct that grants them their elite status.

I don't want to look at this anymore than need be. The world is full of people with small minds and little knowledge, who by virtue of their huge egos, are certain they should be in control of all the resources and the telling of others what to do. It is a world that is forever out of control; that always has been and always will be, and it seems that it is mostly run by narrow minded, short sighted people who can only ever create more problems than they solve. The *Tao Teh Ching* states very eloquently that,

When the common people are starving,
it is because of over taxation.
Politicians get fat
by padding their pockets with a working man's sweat.

When the common people become rebellious
it is because of overbearing government.
When the government becomes extreme
the people begin to laugh at death.

By courting extremes, one invites death.
In following The Way,
one chooses everlasting life.

If I sound a bit disillusioned with the world it's because I am. Anyone who looks clearly into the nature of bureaucracy and the mechanisms of group think would be. In an authentic search for spiritual truth, all of one's energy must be allocated toward breaking through one's personal mental and emotional limitations. In the pursuit of the highest goal of nondual consciousness there can be no spare energy for involving one's self in politics. Politics is a bottomless quagmire that can only ever divert one's energy from the final goal of truth realization. The attempt to reform the world for the better is one the most admirable of causes on a relative level. But ultimately you cannot fix something that is by its very nature designed to be forever out of control. Duality is not something that can be rectified by focusing on the external divisions. It can only be rectified internally, one person at a time, through the process of a most rigorous personal examination.

Fixing the world, creating Shangri-la for humanity, is one of the most enticing sideshows that Maya can offer a well meaning individual. "Go ahead and try it," Maya will tell you. "Without your help, we will never be able to create paradise on earth." And so you'll run head first into the fray, waving a banner that says something or another. Your battle cry will be loud and fierce, at least for a short while. Keep on that path and you'll wake up one day dried up, old, bitter and feeling that your life has been a complete waste. It is supremely difficult to break through one's own rigid mental constructs. How much less likely is it that you could break through and reform a massive and dense collective construct like the government?

It is through the realization of nondual consciousness that an individual truly succeeds in creating the utmost benefit for humanity, not through politics. Nondual consciousness itself is the realization of your own personal Shangri-la regardless of the circumstances of the world, the nation, the state, the city, the family; regardless of even your own personal socioeconomic fluctuations. Abide in nondual consciousness and the universe is set right. Far from becoming a burden to the world, a truth realized person demonstrates the pinnacle of human potential and uplifts the consciousness of all of humanity in a silent, humble and powerful way. It is not by focusing on division and external "problems," but by realizing the perfection of the universe *as it is* that one helps usher in the most potent and final resolution of all of the worlds so called "problems".

It is the world of duality itself that is the problem. That's the hilarious recurring joke in this mad sitcom. Extending our energies into and believing in the problems of the world only strengthens their reality. This isn't denial. It is a total shift of paradigm to see reality from the most all inclusive view. If you look at the world from outer space you'll see this wonderful blue planet tilted perfectly at 23.5 degrees, revolving around the sun in a dance of perfection. Likewise, if you look at the atoms and subatomic particles that comprise the universe, it becomes apparent that everything is moving with a perfect precision that is ridiculous to attempt to deny. It is only at a certain level of focus that we can look at people and situations and deem them as problematic. This is the aim of Maya: to keep us firmly focused on the superficial level that appears as the imperfect and transient world of duality.

Imagine you are watching a pedestrian get hit by a bus. It would be disturbing to say the least. Now imagine rewinding the scene and watching it from the level of subatomic particles. All you would see is the shifting of protons and electrons. There would be no horror; no emotion whatsoever. Watching the shifting of protons and electrons, it would be hard to differentiate any part of the scene as intrinsically good or bad. I imagine there has never been a scientist researching sub atomic particles that has believed that the particles were capable of misbehaving or suffering in any way. I can only imagine what that would be like.

> "It is a total shift of paradigm to see reality from the most all inclusive view."

"Hey Hal, you've gotta come here and take a look at this," says Stanley pointing at the atomic microscope.

"What is it?" Hal asks bending down to look.

"You see that," says Stanley, "that atom is unhappy with its chemical element. It's ordered the execution of those protons over there in order to reach a more stable state. And look over there! Those protons are protesting and organizing a militia to overthrow the atom!"

"Well I'll be dammed!" says Hal. "Subatomic particles are human after all!"

Ridiculous as it sounds, this is what we all do. We foist our opinions and emotions on reality and decide that we alone know what is best for ourselves and the world. We are like masses of protons, electrons and neutrons that have been trained against all odds, to be judgmental and opinionated. We spend our emotional energy wishing the configuration of atoms and sub atomic particles could be like it was in the past, or hoping that they will adopt a particular shape in the future. We are in the final analysis however, just temporary masses of atoms and subatomic particles that have been personified and taught by Maya how to dream in the duality of time. Beyond that duality, we are consciousness itself: the very stuff that atoms and subatomic particles are made out of. We cannot be created or destroyed and all transitions are equal from the all inclusive view of nondual consciousness.

The world and its nations all have their own cycles and issues to work through. Good times have always been followed by bad times and bad times will always be followed by good. Likewise, as individuals, we have our own cycles, patterns and issues to deal with. Inward is always the most useful direction for any authentic spiritual journey. It is what is immediately within reach. Solving our own problems by transcending duality once and for all is the only real solution for humanity and the world. We can't go back to a golden age of civilization as a nation anymore than I can wish myself back to the safety of Grandpa Hoffman's dining room table. Likewise, even if and when a new golden age does transpire for all of humanity it will be transient. This is how it is: the only truth to be found lies not in the world of duality, but within ourselves and within this moment. Find that; find nondual consciousness and all will be right with the world.

CHAPTER TWELVE

Nirvana for Numbskulls

SMOKE AND ASH

Truth calls to us
from the depths of a silent heart.
Unpretentious and alone
we must unravel this most compelling mystery.
Surrendered, let's hold vigil
stoking this fire from the inside out.
Let's peer into this flame until we are entirely consumed.
Ego masks burn around a flame like this,
but for some, the appeal is too great to be denied.
We are like curious little puppets playing with fire:
it only hurts until we've turned to smoke and ash.

Now that I've talked about the majority of ways that Maya likes to sidetrack you from lasting happiness, let's start exploring the fastest way to discover it. The first thing to begin looking at on your journey toward nondual consciousness is your thoughts. Self-enquiry is a process of continually examining the nature of your conscious experience and it begins with your thoughts.

Begin to study your mind with the detachment of a good scientist. What kinds of thoughts tend to recur for you on a day to day basis? Are they thoughts of the future or the past? These are some of the first thoughts to deal with as nondual consciousness must be had in the here and now. It is a common concern among people new to self-enquiry that if they don't think about and plan for the future, everything will fall apart. If we examine this notion closely however, we will notice that even our most meticulously thought out plans have something at their root: consciousness. Consciousness is the mother. Without consciousness you could have no ideas or thoughts whatsoever. Thoughts of and plans for the future are simply limited attempts to guide consciousness toward a desired outcome in time. Witness your thoughts about the future impartially and pay attention to where they spring from and to where they return. Continually question yourself, *who is it that is having these thoughts*? It is this act of internal witnessing and enquiring with one pointed focus that will eventually stabilize as nondual consciousness.

"It is a common concern among people new to self-enquiry that if they don't think about and plan for the future, everything will fall apart."

If you can go beyond your thoughts of the future and rest in the consciousness that creates them, you will find that far from things falling apart, your life will begin to take on a spontaneous design that is free, open ended and unmistakably coherent. This can take a bit of faith in the beginning, as your mind—Maya—will undoubtedly rebel at your scrutiny. Your mind will tell you that if you refuse to listen to it and heed it, that your life will definitely become a shambles. If you're doing it right though, you will also scrutinize the fearful thoughts that come up in response to your initial enquiry, objectively and without feeding them further emotion. It is Maya that perpetuates the fear thoughts. She needs you to take her bait and bite her hook with the teeth of your emotion. Once you do however, she will tow you along like a big mouth bass until you remember to unclench your mental jaws. This is the essence of self-enquiry. You witness your thoughts and track them to the silence that resides in the center of consciousness from where they spring. Over time, the thoughts will revert to longer and longer periods of residing in the pure silence of nondual consciousness. It is simple, but not easy. Watch the thoughts that flitter in and out of your consciousness, but do not push at them, hold onto them or chase after them. Try and remain steadfastly in the center of the pure consciousness that underlies all transient thoughts.

Work on this for awhile. Be easy on yourself when you find that despite your best efforts at detachment and self-enquiry, you're still taking the bait over and over again. Maya is an expert at feeding similar thoughts with countless variations directly into your thought stream. If you get down on yourself for taking the bait you will only be feeding Maya with more emotion. Just let go of the bait, and then let go of the negative thoughts that follow the realization that you've been hooked yet again. Shake it off. Laugh a little bit. Tell Maya she's a naughty girl and shake your finger at her, then go about with your self-enquiry.

Thoughts of the past and regret thoughts are the flipside of future thoughts. We dial into painful scenarios of the past with the mistaken idea that if we only watch them, if we only replay them over and over again, somehow they will be healed. This is just another wiggly worm that Maya is trying to feed you. When you see thoughts of the past coming up; when you feel the regret of deeds done in the past, recognize them for what they are and then let them go. Come back to the present. If there's something that needs to be done to rectify situations past, realize that those things will be done when the time is right. Only from the vantage point of this moment will you begin to find your closure. When you've reconciled yourself internally the external will naturally follow. Internal peace and contentment will eventually lead to the resolution of all external problems.

No matter what it was that transpired in the past, no matter how egregiously you were wronged, or how egregiously you wronged another, realize that it was meant to be and move on. Again, closure will be had when the time is right, but closure must begin by removing your emotional energy from past regrets. It is a basic realization of nondual consciousness that nothing can transpire that is not the will of Mother Consciousness.

There are an infinite amount of factors that must combine to produce even a single life event and they are completely beyond our comprehension. To think that anything could have transpired other than the way it did is a complete waste of energy. If you think that something happened in the past that did not transpire perfectly, you are essentially saying that God messed something up. Tell your mind to shut it. God is in charge of everything.

Take whatever lessons were learned from past events and move on. When you recognize past thoughts or regret thoughts, let them go and continue with your self-enquiry. If you look behind you you'll notice that it is Maya that is dropping these thoughts into your head, hoping to get a reaction out of you. When you face her she'll blush and shrug her shoulders as if to say, "What? I wasn't doing anything."

Tell her you've got to go. Tell her you're working on abiding in nondual consciousness. She might get a little huffy at first, but she'll find something else to do. After all, she has roughly 7 billion other fish on this planet to throw bait at and nearly 500,000 more being born every day. Tell her she doesn't need you anymore. Tell her it's been fun but you've outgrown her. Tell her you're just not moving in the same direction anymore. You're like 99% inward and only 1% outward. Tell her it's not her it's you. Remind her of what an awesome goddess of delusion she is and how sorry you are that the time has come to part ways.

"Maya," you'll say, "I'm like only 1% a duality person and like 99% a nondual consciousness person, so I just can't be with you anymore."

When you've gone beyond thoughts of the future and the past and are resting in the moment, start taking a look at your thoughts about identity. Do you still think you're someone in particular, someone special? How tied into age, heritage, family role, religion or career are you? All these things can be hang ups and can obstruct you from a clear experience of nondual consciousness. Your career and family role are only a small part in the grand play of Maya. They are only temporary descriptions of what consciousness is doing through you at any given moment. What happens if your career tanks? How upset will you be? Will you feel empty when your kids have grown up and moved away? Is your identity strongly tied into what kind of husband or wife you are? Look at the thoughts that tie you into your particular roles. Are they thoughts of pride or superiority? Or do you feel bad because you don't think you've done a good enough job in a particular role? How big of an issue is your sexual orientation? Are you really tied into being straight or gay as an important aspect of your identity? Watch these thoughts the same way you would watch future and past thoughts. When a thought comes up regarding your identity, ask yourself *to whom do these thoughts come*? Look closely at your answers. Who do you think you are? When you ask yourself "Who am I?" there can be no final answer. What you are is consciousness pure and simple. Any other answer or description is temporary and for the purposes of abiding in nondual consciousness, should not be given much importance.

Go ahead and ask yourself the question: "Who am I?" See if Maya

"When you've gone beyond thoughts of the future and the past and are resting in the moment, start taking a look at your thoughts about identity."

isn't standing there beckoning and beseeching you to read from her cue cards.

"Why, you're Jane Doe of course!" she'll say. "You're an ace of a lawyer, a supermom, your stock portfolio is worth X amount of dollars and you have the best abs in your yoga class! And don't you forget it sister!"

But you have to forget it. Be whatever it is you are in the moment, but don't ruminate over it and get too tied into it. One day your abs will be old and shriveled and hanging in ghastly folds over your waistline. One day you'll die and your stock portfolio will be worth exactly nothing to you. If you're going to have an ultimate goal why not reach for what is eternal?

Have faith that your duties will be taken care of efficiently, even as you go beyond your roles and identity markers. Question your thoughts relentlessly until they dissolve into pure silence, then blow Maya a kiss, give her a wink and a wave her goodbye. You won't fail to do your job adequately because of practicing self-enquiry. On the contrary, when you've gone beyond yourself and your identity roles, you'll have more energy and awareness with which to accomplish those tasks you are meant to accomplish. Clarifying your consciousness can only ever lead to good things, even though in the beginning it may appear as if things are going relatively worse. When you really get into an authentic spiritual path Maya *will* try to upset you. Hang on and simply observe negative life situations. No matter how bad or good a situation appears, don't feed it energy.

When you've gone a certain distance with your self-enquiry, you may be surprised to find that you're in a role that you don't really find satisfying and that you never wanted to be in at all.

"Oh crap!" you'll say, "Now I get it. I became an accountant because my dad pressured me into being a business major in college! No wonder I hate this job!" Then you'll open your office window and fling your pocket protector full of pens as far as you can with gleeful abandon, knowing that a more enjoyable existence awaits you beyond that role. Perhaps you were meant to do something more creative than what you are doing now. Your creative energy will become free and open when you go beyond the limitations of your mind into pure consciousness itself.

As you examine your thoughts and ideas, begin to pay attention to the emotions that accompany them. You'll notice that many of the thoughts and ideas that you experience on a day to day basis have a particular emotional component associated with them. Start paying attention to what those emotions feel like. Watch them as you would your thoughts; see where the emotions come from, where they reside and to where they return. Perhaps when you think about finances you begin to feel fear or worry in your chest or in the pit of your stomach. As we saw in the chapter "Mo' Money," this is one of Maya's most obvious games. As we saw in the chapter "Return to Shangri-La," wealth distribution is quite uneven in many parts of the world and has been since the beginning of civilization. This is one of the biggest dichotomies that Maya utilizes to entrench us in the world of duality. She loves to keep people tied into ideas of lack and limitation, or conversely, the endless frenzy to accumulate more and more. Finances are very deeply associated with most people's identities and they are undoubtedly associated with some heavy duty emotions like fear, envy, anger, greed, entitlement or pride.

How do you feel when you think about your finances? Is there any emotional charge there? Financial fears are very directly linked with the Grand Poobah of all fears: the fear of death. As you examine your emotions closely, you will sooner or later come upon the fear of death or the fear of non-existence. Most of our smaller fears, phobias, cravings and desires are linked with this pervasive underlying fear. The mind is ever trying to solidify the ego mask in an attempt to fabricate the feeling of safety in a temporary, illusory world.

If you look into your feelings about finances and notice that there is any remaining charge there, ask yourself, *who is it that feels this way?* Probe into the emotion and see what else boils up as you examine it closely. When you go beyond emotions about finances you'll notice that in nondual consciousness, there is a simple knowing that all is well and everything will be fine. If you can just oust your fears and abide in nondual consciousness, circumstances will likely move to support your existence quite naturally. When you are abiding in nondual consciousness it won't even matter if they don't. When you experience yourself as pure consciousness itself, external circumstances will not concern you much. Mother Consciousness doesn't set you up to fail though. It is only your thoughts and emotions that keep you pushing and pulling on the world and that keep the ego mask mired in endless karmic patterns. It is Maya that is creeping up next to you whispering the fear thoughts or the greed thoughts into your ear. Next time you turn and catch her doing it, tell her you're just not going to buy it anymore. Tell her you'd rather starve to death in the street with a smile on your face than lay curled up in a ball worrying about money. Or if you're already rich, tell her you have enough and give the excess to charities or people in need. Maya might become a bit forlorn when you go beyond the games of wealth and poverty, as you will be taking away one of her very favorite ploys. But don't get to feeling sorry for her just yet, she's got plenty more tricks up her sleeve.

"If you can just oust your fears and abide in nondual consciousness, circumstances will likely move to support your existence quite naturally."

Maybe financial fears aren't really your thing. You've been there, done that, your portfolio is all spic and span; or better yet, you've become neutral about finances altogether. What other kinds of emotions do you perceive in your daily experience? As you look into your consciousness more and more, all kinds of things will begin to rise to the surface; things you had buried, things you had forgotten, things that you didn't even know were there. They will all come boiling up violently at a certain point. You'll have to brace yourself when the ego begins to rail and you start to get an up close look at the ridiculous and monstrous ego mask.

Perhaps like me, you will have some event or series of events that set you on a rampage for truth. Maybe a whole bunch of things will start going wrong for you at the same time. Perhaps you'll wake one morning to find your hair thinning and be thrust into a mid-life crisis. Before you go running out to buy a red Ferrari and a toupee', let's take a closer look at the nature of adverse circumstances. Tragedies and adverse circumstances used in the correct fashion can give us a fantastic amount of impetus for uncovering nondual consciousness. The formula is simple. When something happens that we are not happy about we can go one of two ways. We can either shake our fist at the sky and yell, "Hey God! Why the hell is this is happening to me? What did I do to deserve such a crap storm?" Or we can do the more sober and productive thing: step back for a minute and question ourselves, *who is it that believes these circumstances are undesirable and why?*

An undesirable circumstance is only undesirable based on the context in which you are looking at it. Most of us are looking at circumstances from the particular position of our ego masks. We get upset when something happens that goes against the stream of our identity and who we think we are. We get angry or disappointed if events don't tally with what we believe we deserve. Whether your adverse circumstances are related to finances, career, health, relationship or even the loss of a loved one, the cause of your discomfort is the same. If you can step back from, or even destroy your ego mask entirely, circumstances will simply become what they are: not good or bad, but perfect.

Without heavy preferences and opinions about outcomes, you could never be really upset regardless of what transpires. So next time you're driving down the street and somebody cuts in front of your brand new red Ferrari, watch the anger. Find out where it comes from. If someone rear ends you and you hit your head on the Italian leather steering wheel sending your toupee' flying into the street, find out who it is that thinks this shouldn't have happened. Whatever the circumstance, your job is to find out who it is that is getting angry, excited or upset about things.

I personally used to get triggered emotionally by bad drivers. Anyone who does enough driving in the Los Angeles area will have plenty of opportunity to practice self-enquiry in regards to driving. When I moved to a much smaller town I thought things would be different and better. I figured everyone would just be all earthy and nature like and courteous. I was wrong. There seem to be just as many inconsiderate and terrible drivers per capita here as there were in L.A. The real difference is that I don't get triggered by them anymore.

Some time ago, Christina and I were heading to the coast for the weekend. We were in a right lane that was soon to be merging with the left lane so I began scanning the scene, looking for the best place to merge. The woman in the left lane, whose turn it should have been to let me in, began speeding up to the bumper of the car in front of her to prevent me from merging. There was enough time and lane left for me to accelerate and get in front of the car in front of her, so I punched it, the turbo kicked in and I got in front of the other car no problem. The car in front of her saw what she was doing and slowed to let me in. The woman in the truck who wouldn't let me in was furious. At the next red light that we came to, the woman in the truck actually got out of her vehicle, walked up to my driver side window and began yelling something or another and shaking her fist. Her face was livid. Just as she was squaring up to my window though the light turned green and I drove on, leaving her there to yell at the empty space where I had just been. I'm sure that must have pissed her off to no end. She was left 25 car lengths back with a honking line of cars behind her before she could make it back into her truck and move. That lady had some serious issues but it never even occurred to me to engage her. What would be the point? She'll face those anger issues again and again until she gets it figured out or has a heart attack.

It's not that I'm an insensitive person, quite the contrary. I love puppies and kitties and my eyes tear up at the poignant moments in dramatic movies. It just doesn't occur to me to engage people's egos anymore. Abiding in nondual consciousness is the epitome of compassion, but it doesn't necessarily look like anything in particular. It is the epitome of compassion because when you have withdrawn all your energy from the world, you are no longer tampering with things or people anymore. You are simply letting people and situations exist as they are, and perhaps subtly influencing things from the depth of nondual consciousness. If you are meant to interact with people in some way it will happen, but it will generally be without any heavy emotion.

Temperatures were running into the 90's that week and it was probably making people crankier than usual. On that very same trip on the way back from the beach, a woman in a mini van launched herself out of a supermarket driveway, across two lanes and into our lane cutting us off with a vengeance and very nearly wrecking into us. I literally had to slam on the brakes to avoid her running directly into the side of the car. We pulled up next to her at the next light and I just glanced over curiously to see who it was that had very nearly wrecked their minivan into my poor little Subaru. There in the driver seat was a very large lady wearing a gaudy mumu decorated with flowers; arms as big as my thighs. She didn't look particularly malevolent but maybe a bit ill humored. Perhaps she never saw me or maybe she just drove with reckless abandon as a habit. Someone in the passenger seat behind her, I can only guess it was her son based on the resemblance, rolled down his window and

"Abiding in nondual consciousness is the epitome of compassion, but it doesn't necessarily look like anything in particular. "

began yelling at me, "What do you want Motherfucker!? Who are you looking at!?" I really didn't want anything, especially from him based on the size of the hand he was flipping me off with, so I just smiled sheepishly and kept driving. That was a funny weekend. Maya was going to great lengths to get a rise out of me so it seemed.

Just as a peculiar side note, I noticed that the further removed I was becoming from personal opinion and emotion, the more bizarre the tactics Maya used to come after me. When I had gotten to a point where the majority of my days were spent in a thought free, nondual consciousness, Maya also began coming after me in my sleep and dreams. I began having dreams that seemed more like real encounters on some kind of astral plane with energetically foreign entities, rather than the normal, airy, ephemeral kinds of dreams I was used to. In those dreams, there was almost always a point at which one of the dream entities would come at me and try to provoke me into anger or fear. In the beginning, the dream entities sometimes succeeded in provoking me into a conflict, or into feelings of anger or fear. But as the dreams continued, I began to watch the provocations with the same neutrality that I was experiencing in daily life. In every successive dream, if I was able to keep from feeding the dream entity with any sort of emotional reaction, the dream would begin to change or I would simply wake up.

At one point I had a lucid dream or astral experience—I don't really differentiate between the two anymore—in which I was just floating around in an energy body. I would come across various scenes and situations, but I kept all my energy focused at my center and just continued floating along gently. After sometime, I found myself in a cement basement where several malevolent beings were looking to harm me. They tried throwing various objects at me but the objects just bounced off as I paid them no attention and had no fear or anger about the situation. Two of the beings then moved toward me and grabbed me by my arms and legs. I was floating in mid air at the time and I was a bit surprised to find out they were capable of grabbing my energy body, but I didn't panic. Their touch felt violent and negative and it seemed as if they were trying to will me into a more tangible state so as to inflict some damage on me. I tried to will myself away, but somehow their intentions kept me in a grounded state and I was unable to escape. I still didn't panic. I told them, "Fine, if you won't let me go I'll just wake myself up and be done with you." I willed myself awake and went about the rest of my night with no emotion.

I wanted to speak to those experiences because I've never really seen mention of anything quite like it in other peoples accounts of spiritual awakening; the one exception being the Buddha's encounters with Mara[9]. I fully recognize that the dream encounters were, like everything else in my experience, just emanations of my own mind. They are emanations in which Maya still tries to draw me into conflict by playing on my emotional triggers. Maya is simply how I like to personify the negative aspects of the personal, dualistic, illusory mind. Interestingly, the conflict energy with which I was confronted by the various dream entities was very nearly identical in quality and feel as the energy that was displayed by both of the angry people in the above mentioned driving incidents. Just as a forewarning, it seems that when you really begin to center yourself in nondual consciousness, Maya might pull out the stops and start flailing at you with a bit of desperation. It is just the purging of the remaining negativity in your own consciousness. Your only job is to witness Maya's flailing and not react.

In your journey toward nondual consciousness, there are larger

---

[9]In Buddhism, Mara is the demon who tempted Gautama Buddha by trying to seduce him with the vision of beautiful women who, in various legends, are often said to be Mara's daughters.[11] In Buddhist cosmology, Mara personifies unskillfulness, the "death" of the spiritual life. He is a tempter, distracting humans from practicing the spiritual life by making the mundane alluring or the negative seem positive.

personal constructs that you will begin to break down as you progress, namely, psychological tendencies and habits; what are referred to in Sanskrit as *samskaras*. Psychological tendencies are conglomerations of mental and emotional patterns that have been congealed over time to form broader personality characteristics. They can be very deeply ingrained and must also be examined thoroughly and without emotion in order to begin to break them down into their component parts.

Are you timid or shy? Are you bold or aggressive? Do you have an addictive personality? Are you lustful or greedy; vindictive perhaps? You have to peer into these broader patterns closely in order to dissect them and break them down into the thoughts and emotions that comprise them. These psychological tendencies are the overall qualities with which we approach and relate to ourselves and the world and that bind us to duality.

Say for instance you have a smoking habit that is the result of an addictive personality. The first thing to do is to simply witness the habit. What are the thoughts and emotions that drive it? Is there a nervousness or fear that is lurking somewhere in the background that you are trying to distract yourself from? Do you feel an emotional void that you are attempting to cover up by virtue of the habit? Maybe it's none of these things. Maybe you just like the rush of the nicotine running through your blood stream into your brain. The main point in dissecting your psychological tendencies is to see if there is something underneath them that has yet to be resolved; to find out if there is any emotional charge left. If there is, then you must uncover that something and scrutinize it closely. Ask yourself, *who is it that still has this emotional charge and where does it come from?* If there isn't any emotional charge there, nothing that you are trying to cover up or run away from, that's great. If you're abiding in nondual consciousness and you just

> "Psychological tendencies are conglomerations of mental and emotional patterns that have been congealed over time to form broader personality characteristics."

want to smoke for the sake of it, I say go for it. Smoke up Johnny. If that is the case however, I imagine the habit would be very light and could be easily taken or left with very little concern.

What holds us in habitual thought patterns, psychological tendencies and habits, is primarily emotion. If say, we are a smoker and we are particularly down on ourselves because of it, that very emotion of self hatred will keep us locked into the pattern even more tightly. Having particularly negative emotions about something only mires you in it more firmly. The way to get beyond addictions or any other psychological tendencies is simply to witness them objectively. Watch the emotions and thoughts that surround the patterns. Examine them thoroughly and impartially and the patterns will begin to disperse. If you don't put any further emotion into a pattern it will eventually lose its strength. Again, you do this through self-enquiry. Watch yourself throughout the day and even into your sleep and dreams if possible. You need to become absolutely familiar with all the aspects of your ego mask, even as you continue to take your energy back from it.

To continue the smoking analogy, it's another of Maya's favorite ploys to talk you into doing something and then turn around and beat you up for it. Maybe you haven't smoked for awhile and you're feeling particularly bored on a Sunday afternoon. You're just kind of sitting around wondering what to do when some ideas start forming in your mind.

"Hey… Psst… hey. Why don't you walk down to the store and get a pack of cigs? After all you haven't smoked for awhile; your wife's out of town; go ahead, you deserve it!" Maya says, giving you a wink.

"No I really shouldn't," you say. "It was hard enough to quit last time."

"Come on, just one won't hurt you. You're not going to live forever anyway," Maya says. "What've you got to lose? You'll feel better you know. It'll be fun!"

"Yeah, you might be right," you say, and you walk to the store for the pack of cigs. You get home, light up a cig and smoke the heck out of it and you're feeling pretty good about things when...

"Hey man," Maya says, "you shouldn't have done that."

"What are you talking about? I thought I was supposed to do it. In fact, I thought you recommended it," you say.

"No way man, you messed up. You're a loser now man."

"Aw crap," you say, "I guess I am kind of a loser. I guess I did mess up."

"Damn right you messed up," Maya says shaking her head in disappointment.

Maya is good cop, bad cop, conspiratorial friend and enemy all rolled into one. She wants you to get emotionally tied into things. She would prefer that you continually rebuild and strengthen your ego mask and its patterns as she knocks them down, rather than finally tearing them apart yourself, once and for all. Further, she'd love for you to go running out into the world with your strong ego mask and to keep upholding her collective ego constructs like society, religion and government.

As far as psychological tendencies go, the good cop/ bad cop guilt game is one of Maya's very favorite ways of roping you into duality, and what ultimately enables her to give you a beat down once you've tied into it. This is a common pattern that she uses to hold all of your psychological tendencies into place. Say for instance you're habitually shy as a pattern. You go to a party and Maya starts telling you it's time to get beyond your shyness. She talks you into going and starting up a conversation with the handsome guy or the pretty girl on the other side of the room. No sooner will you be across the room introducing yourself, than Maya will start telling you what an idiot you are for having done it. She'll probably even get your palms to perspire and make you stutter while you're making your move.

"Hi, my name's Eu...Eu...Eugene!" you'll say, as you accidentally trip and spill your beer all over the pretty girl's designer purse. Maya, you see, has a morose penchant for humiliating physical comedy.

Psychological tendencies or samskaras, are not inherently good or bad. It's only the energy that we feed into them that binds us to them and holds them in place. Even someone who is abiding in nondual consciousness will have apparent psychological tendencies that appear to be playing themselves out. The difference is that such a person will not be tied into them, and consequently, they will be very light.

Utilize self-enquiry to go beyond your psychological tendencies. The process is the same. Recognize the patterns and then look at them closely until you start to uncover the thoughts and emotions that hold them in place. What kinds of patterns do you have and what are you getting out of them? Are your tendencies a protective measure? Do you use them to shield you from disappointment, fear or loneliness? How strong are the thoughts and emotions that drive them? Again, ask yourself, *who is it that has these psychological tendencies and where do they come from?* Keep probing into them until you again revert to the silent nondual consciousness that resides beneath all thoughts and emotions. Ironically our psychological tendencies, just like the entirety of the ego mask, are put in place for the purpose of personal protection and in order to facilitate a sense of well being. Like all thoughts and emotions however; like all mental constructs, psychological tendencies are temporary and our job is to go beyond them. All mental constructs and psychological tendencies are ultimately gimmicks that Maya uses to distract us from real spiritual awakening.

One particular psychological tendency worth examining more closely is worldly ambition. Ambition is lauded in modern society and most people are trained at a very early age with the idea that they need to go out and grab life by the horns. People, so we learn, derive their worth from what they do and how much they own. We are taught that our desires and ambitions are paramount and that we must go forth boldly to fulfill them. Perhaps we even take on the hopes and ambitions of our parents or society at large if our personal ambitions aren't grand enough on their own.

"We have high hopes for you Johnny!" our parents tell us before we've even learned how to walk.

Ask a five year old child what they would like to be when they grow up and you'll get a variety of answers. You'll hear things like a fireman, an astronaut, president of the United States, professional athlete and the like. Very few five-year-olds will tell you it is their ambition to be a janitor or a garbage man and almost none will say their ambition is to become enlightened. Most of us are taught at an early age that modern society is divided up sharply into winners and losers. As a consequence of this psychological division, many of us go striving for a station in life that will give us clout, a high income and the approval of our relatives and peers. Ambition should be looked at closely because it will help you to determine what it is you are truly looking for in this lifetime. If a five year old told their parents that their greatest ambition is to abide in nondual consciousness, their parents would likely be very concerned.

> "It is crucial in the pursuit of nondual consciousness that uncovering Absolute Reality be your number one priority."

This is however, the greatest ambition of all, even though it has little to do with worldly success. If you're reading this book, to some extent you agree. It is crucial in the pursuit of nondual consciousness that uncovering Absolute Reality be your number one priority. Anything less will bring you only mediocre results. I've met many people on a "spiritual path" that don't have any clear idea of what it is that they're looking for or where they're headed. They "meditate" for a half hour a day and then spend the rest of their time doing everything in their power to distract themselves from the reality of the moment. Consequently, spiritual practice for them is just a routine and an ideal that doesn't really lead to anything discernible. For them, spiritual practice is just another "doing" and therefore just another distraction from truth. Many people are still trying to accrue merit so as to go to heaven or have better karma in their next life. I say why wait? There is no better karma or heaven than the one that exists for you in this very moment within your true nature.

So what is it that you really want out of life? Ask yourself and listen to the answers that come up very clearly. If nondual consciousness— enlightenment—is first and foremost on your bucket list, you're on the fast track to Absolute Reality. If anything else whatsoever tops that list, I've got to tell you, you might as well go for that instead. You will not find abiding nondual consciousness if your priority is to become the governor or mayor of your town.

Go for the gusto; go for broke, and the rest of life's details will work themselves out. This doesn't mean you have to quit your job and go sit in a cave full time. On the contrary, self-enquiry can be practiced whatever your life situation. When you obtain clarity of consciousness you will realize that you are existing in the perfect circumstances at all times whatever they may be. Say for instance you are in an abusive relationship or another negative life circumstance; if you continue pursuing nondual consciousness wholeheartedly, something will necessarily shift and your circumstances will certainly change in response to your firm abidance in the absolute peace at the center of consciousness. It is purely physics. If you can remain at the center of life, in nondual consciousness, the world, other people, Maya, will have no more power over you. Worldly people will become absolutely bored with you because you are no longer feeding the world with your energy. They will go away accordingly, leaving you to your spiritual practice and abiding peace and happiness. Earlier I said that if you abide in nondual consciousness you will begin drawing other nondual people into your life. This is how it is. Like attracts like, and people can only really stand to be around others of a similar level of consciousness for any length of time. Work on the absolute truth of your own existence and *everything* else in your life will sort itself out.

There is absolutely nothing to worry about. Call it destiny if you will, but you have a specific pattern to work out in your life and in this world and it will undoubtedly be fulfilled. It is my experience that Mother Consciousness holds the tally exactly. She is capable of running absolutely everything and your only real job is to find her and abide with her in this moment. Trust Mother Consciousness and pursue your self-enquiry unrelentingly. In due course you will find yourself poised in the experience of a freedom you could have never imagined. Freedom, total and complete is your true birthright, but it must be steadfastly uncovered until you actually experience firm abidance in the center of pure, nondual consciousness. Ideas and philosophies about freedom are cheap trinkets compared to the real deal. If you're ready to get down to business you've got to roll up your sleeves and get your hands dirty with this stuff. You've got to keep going within and digging until you couldn't stop if you tried. Thorough introspection through self-enquiry is the key. Used correctly and unrelentingly, it will allow you to transcend the elegant charade and unlock the innermost truth of existence. In this truth you will find what you've always been searching for and what has always been there all along. When you abide in nondual consciousness steadfastly, life will become increasingly pleasant as the illusion of duality melts into the ever present experience of Absolute Reality.

CHAPTER THIRTEEN

The Nondual Manifesto

LIFE IS FOR . . .

Life is for stretching out this moment
under the canopy of truth
until it replaces time.
Heaven is dissolving into eternity;
perceiving only unity
where once there had been two.
Who can ever explain
why everyone doesn't love completely?
What words could ever suffice
to return multiplicity
back to the source?
People move in circles
and life spins on unceasingly,
but truth lies through this tiny gate
that nobody can fit through.

1. Everything serves Mother Consciousness. Not a thing exists that is beyond her control.

2. Everything serves Mother Consciousness. Her will exists alone.

3. Mother Consciousness holds the reigns. You are a spark while she is the fire. She accomplishes everything. You only appear to exist.

4. Do not be so bold as to think anything has ever gone wrong. Do not be so blind as to think there is any such thing as failure.

5. Do not be so ignorant as to think your thoughts are original. Even denial of Mother Consciousness is through her power alone.

6. Life and death have no intrinsic meaning. Mother Consciousness is the absolute truth. Do not be so naive as to think of worldly life as real.

7. Mother Consciousness holds the tally. You are a leaf on her universal breeze. All things go her way. Stop your mind and see if it's so.

8. Mother Consciousness is the Ultimate: The Way, The Truth and The Life. She is the alpha and the omega. You and she are ONE.

9. Mother Consciousness is benevolence itself. She brings all things and beings into life. She cares for them and nurtures them whether or not they accept her love.

10. Mother Consciousness knows your pain. Give it to her and she'll take it away. Mother Consciousness knows your joy. Give that to her as well.

11. Mother Consciousness has no regrets. Take her example and lose yours as well. Mother Consciousness knows only freedom. Surrender to her and be free.

12. Mother Consciousness transcends time. There is this moment and this moment alone. If you wish to surrender to her, it must be done in the NOW.

13. Mother Consciousness knows not defeat. Every ending is simply another beginning. Go beyond beginnings and endings. Find eternity at the center of life.

14. Mother Consciousness is your disciple. Understand this and all else is won. Mother Consciousness is your master. You and she are the same.

15. Mother Consciousness is incapable of hate. She is love itself. Take her example in relationships, let all transgressions be void.

16. Mother Consciousness is the Trinity: The Mother, Son and Holy Ghost. Do not believe you are separate. That is the only sin that exists.

17. Mother Consciousness is total perfection. By extension you are perfection as well. Go beyond your thoughts and emotions until you know yourself as divine.

18. Mother Consciousness knows what is right. She knows that there is nothing wrong. Divest yourself of all bias. Trust her and all is well.

19. Mother Consciousness owns the universe. She guarantees that

you will always have a place. Be at home in this moment and know you are where you are meant to be.

20. Mother Consciousness is the ultimate. She is the substratum of all that exists. Her silence is absolutely final: you have never been alone.

21. You will never be alone. You have never not existed. You can never cease to exist. You are universal truth itself.

22. Mother Consciousness has a dream and in that dream you're the star. The entire universe will throw flowers at your feet the moment that you transcend separation.

23. Mother Consciousness has a dream. It is your dream as well. Everything you know emanates from your mind. The perfection of this is complete.

24. Mother Consciousness has no purpose. Her art is spontaneous design. The universe is her masterpiece, but only when experienced AS IT IS.

Afterword

"Nondual consciousness isn't anything 'special' in the final analysis; at least it shouldn't be. It seems that we are all meant to be poised sooner or later, on the edge of this very second, peering around and seeing only emptiness, freedom and eternity spanning in every direction."

As I sit here editing this manuscript I can only wonder and be amazed at the nature of consciousness. Nondual consciousness is open ended and lends itself to a sense of freedom and well being that I haven't really felt since I was a child. Everything seems increasingly clear to me now; more than that, it seems absolutely immaculate. Somehow I've always known that this is how people were meant to exist, and so I've moved towards this nondual experience consciously and unconsciously for as long as I can remember.

Nondual consciousness isn't anything "special" in the final analysis; at least it shouldn't be. It seems that we are all meant to be poised sooner or later, on the edge of this very second, peering around and seeing only emptiness, freedom and eternity spanning in every direction. It's the illusions that hold us back from this experience that are the true marvel. Maya weaves a fabrication that is so deceptive, and that alternates between appealing and appalling so convincingly, that it has the power at every turn to take our awareness away from that which is most basic, apparent and always nearer than near.

> "Utilized correctly, and with the tool of self-enquiry in hand, all experiences are stepping stones to the highest plateau of totality."

Life has settled down for me considerably since my one year upheaval. I'm not sure if one year is a normal time frame for the sort of unraveling process I underwent. In reality, everything that has ever transpired in my life has led me up to this moment, so it's impossible to quantify or to generalize about what the process should look like for anyone else. It will be different for each person. What I can say for certain is that every ounce of pain and turmoil that you will ever suffer in your life will be resolved in the unassailable experience and freedom of nondual consciousness. Whatever your life circumstances have been, they were meant to be. Utilized correctly, and with the tool of self-enquiry in hand, all experiences are stepping stones to the highest plateau of totality. Have faith in yourself and know that you are an infinite being in a perfect universe. Mother Consciousness has you firmly in her embrace no matter how convincingly Maya ever tries to show you otherwise.

I am undoubtedly lucky in that I am privileged to have a mate whose spiritual compass is dialed directly beyond the world of illusion as firmly as is mine. We have leaned on each other and learned from each other tremendously on our voyage; but we have only succeeded together because we are, each of us, always looking within *ourselves* for the truth.

My father-in-law Greg has mellowed quite a bit in his views as we've sat around on quite a few weekends discussing the nature of consciousness. He understands where I'm coming from more clearly than before and is striving to find his own truth in his own way. Since his retirement, Greg still continues to find a multitude of activities to occupy himself in all over the United States. He is still on a mission, and a man with a righteous plan. Christina and I have fondly bestowed on him the nickname, "The Scheduler". He is booked out until next year and even has a three week trek to India penciled into his agenda. On his trip he plans to visit many a holy site including a three day stay in Tiruvannamalai, India, where he will visit Ramanasramam and the sacred hill Arunachala. If he is successful, Greg will understand that what he is looking for has always been in the center of his own consciousness, somewhere just beyond his mind, and that that something can be had here and now just as readily as in any other country, holy site or temple.

Without acknowledging the existence of nondual consciousness as one's true nature, I would imagine that many a seeker has failed to find what they were looking for in India. They would fly for twenty five hours only to be presented with a plethora of pollution and to feel the press of peddlers and beggars all around them. Perhaps they would contract the infamous "stomach bug" of India and spend several days curled up in a ball and hunched over a toilet, wondering if enlightenment might be found just on the other side of their gastrointestinal suffering.

All kidding aside, I would like to take a moment to pay homage to one of my most revered teachers. I credit Ramana Maharshi for making the tool of self-enquiry popular and accessible to the public in the last century, and for that, no amount of thanks can be sufficient. On the other hand, Ramana Maharshi himself would be the first to tell you that the greatest thanks you could ever render to the guru is your own self realization. This I have endeavored to do with all my heart and soul.

I would be remiss if I didn't also acknowledge my other most highly esteemed role model: Robert Adams. Robert Adams was a truth realized American teacher who most recently lived and taught in Southern California and in Sedona, Arizona before his passing in the mid 1990's. Robert's teachings are chronicled in his book *Silence of the Heart*. I was lucky enough to find Robert's book and to stumble across some recorded talks of Robert's *satsangs* when I most needed them on my journey. Listening to those talks, along with the practice of one pointed self-enquiry, sharpened the longing for truth that had too long lay dormant in my consciousness. Though I had practiced self-enquiry somewhat halfheartedly for many years, it wasn't until my life began to fall apart that the tools I had been given served me most faithfully. I have emerged from my one year cataclysm completely reborn. With that said, I realize that a thorough dismantling of the ego is only the first step in what appears initially to be a gradual process. Once the ego has been annihilated, consciousness will tend to teeter on the outskirts of the dualistic world unsteadily until at last, it gets pulled into the heart: into nondual consciousness completely. This is where I currently reside: standing on the brink of eternity, tossing the last fragments of my ego mask into the void; waiting for the moment where everything

"...take up this most courageous journey inward toward what you have always been searching for: your true nature..."

goes utterly still and I am called into Absolute Reality entirely.

Although I never met Ramana or Robert, at least not on the physical plane, I now experience their truth more fully and completely than I ever could have prior to my own ego dismantling. Through the grace of Mother Consciousness, their teachings have reached across time and space to point me toward what I had always been looking for. Like any good student I was not to be pacified just with their words alone. I took their cue and began to tear through all my concepts and ideas and even the teachings themselves, until I was left squarely facing the one thing that had held me back all along: my own mind. I offer you this book in the same vein: with the intent that you will go beyond the words and take up this most courageous journey inward, toward what you have always been searching for: your true nature—nondual consciousness—abidance in Absolute Reality.

—Michael T. Ness

About the Author

At the apex of an unfocused 20 year spiritual journey, Michael T. Ness found himself plunged into the depths of a personal and mental crisis that left him reeling and desperate for an effective and final solution to personal suffering. The tool that he found most practical in his time of need was self-enquiry: the cornerstone of the path of Jnana Marga.

To visit M. T. Ness' website and participate in his discussion blog, where relevant topics and questions about self-enquiry, Advaita Vedanta, and the path of Jnana Marga, are regularly discussed, please go to: www.JnanaMargaSociety.com

Aperion Books

Book Publishing for the Digital Age

Aperion Books is dedicated to producing high quality publications that help people facilitate positive change in their lives. We specialize in publishing titles on spirituality, wellness, and personal growth.

Our unique Collaborative Publishing Program is specifically designed to help writers and authors expand their personal and professional horizons through creatively designed books that are distributed to national wholesalers and leading retailers.

www.ingramcontent.com/pod-product-compliance
Lightning Source LLC
LaVergne TN
LVHW011240080426
835509LV00005B/563